Bill Nelson
Outdoorsman Extraordinaire

Compiled by
Sherm Blom

Copyright 2004 by Sherm Blom

ISBN 1-931291-40-3

Published in the United States of America

First Edition, First Printing

Publishing Consultant: Stoneydale Press Publishing Company, 523 Main Street, Stevensville, Montana 59870
Phone: 406-777-2729
Email: stoneydale@montana.com

THE AUTHOR

Sherm Blom was raised on a farm in southern MN and grew up trapping for bounty and fur on his school-day traplines during the 1950s and 1960s. He attended college, studying wildlife biology. During the summers, he worked for the MN Department of Natural Resources, trapping and banding ducks. During the falls, he continued to fur-trap on weekends and during vacations. After trapping season, he worked part-time for a fur-hide-wool buyer. He ran his first all-season professional trapline in 1969. He moved to MT in 1971, attended a guide and packer school, and worked as a big-game guide and packer, fur trapper, and ranch worker for 6 years. He was employed as a government and private predator control trapper in MT, WY, & ID from 1977-1986. He then transferred to the USDA Denver Wildlife Research Center in CO as a research trapper for 5 years. In 1991, he transferred to the USDA Pocatello Supply Depot in Pocatello, ID and became manager in 1996. He retired in 2003 and is traveling throughout the country in a RV.

The author with a #4 Victor underspring trap and a L.C. Smith doublebarrel 12-gauge shotgun that belonged to Bill Nelson and were given to him by Sonny Hootman and Don Paul respectively.

TABLE OF CONTENTS

Acknowledgments 1

Identification of other people mentioned throughout the book 2

Introduction 3

Chapter 1: **Boyhood And The Early Years** 7

Chapter 2: **North To Minnesota** 19

Chapter 3: **Surviving The Depression** 24

Chapter 4: **The Wildcrafter** 26
    Root Digging 27
    Flower Gardening 30
    Shelling 30
    Pearling 33

Chapter 5: **West To California** 39
    Trapping On Foot In The Coastal Ranges 40
    Working For The U.S. Forest Service 43
    Vacation Prospect Lines 44
    Skiing For Sierra Sables 50
    Epilogue 59

Chapter 6: **Marten Lore And Trapping** 62

Chapter 7: **Back To Iowa** 68

Chapter 8: **Aggressive Advertising** 77

Chapter 9: **The Fisherman** 95
    Catfishing 95
    Carp Fishing 99
    Musky Fishing 100
    Trout Fishing In The Sierras 101

Chapter 10: **Montana Prospect Line** 103

Chapter 11: **Bounty Trapping** 106

Chapter 12: **Back To Montana, But Not For Long** 110

Chapter 13: **The Hunter** 112

Chapter 14: **The Trapper** 115
        Fox Trapping 116
        Mink Trapping 117
        Coyote Trapping 119
        Bobcat Trapping 121
        Otter Trapping 122
        Wolf Trapping 123
        Cougar Trapping 124
        Dirt Antifreeze Method 125
        Releasing Skunks, Alive, From Traps
          Without Them Spraying and Without
          Chemical Immobilization 126

Chapter 15: **Trapping Systems And Philosophies** 128

Chapter 16: **Fur Handling And Marketing** 135

Chapter 17: **The Instructor** 140

Chapter 18: **The Author** 141

Chapter 19: **Sayings, Phrases, And Bullet Words** 159

Chapter 20: **The Naturalist And Student** 161

Chapter 21: **The Luremaker** 166

Chapter 22: **The Man** 175

Chapter 23: **Final Chapter** 185

Chapter 24: **Epilogue** 186

ACKNOWLEDGMENTS

I greatly appreciate the generosity, help, and contributions of the following individuals with information, personal experiences, articles, letters, manuscripts, photos, lure bottles, etc. regarding Bill Nelson. Without them, I could not have even attempted this venture. I had lost all of my letters from Bill and the photos I had taken of him and Edith in a fire in 1974. It is very hard to recall and write about someone who has been dead for over 30 years, and I was amazed at the recall of those I interviewed. Bill obviously left a lasting impression on them. If I omitted anyone, I sincerely apologize. I tried to keep track of all the contributors, but after all these years, I may have inadvertently omitted someone. It certainly was not intentional. Many thanks to: Jack Harris, Gus Gehlhar, Don Paul, Sonny Hootman, Harry and Bill Batten, Marlene Rider, Ruth Peterson, John Barbee, George Bryant, Ed Myers, Walt Jacoby, Fuller and Ruth (deceased) Laugeman, Norita from the "LEADER-RECORD," Rick Black (deceased), Bill Waterman(deceased), Richard Schalow (deceased), Josh Lindeman, Rich Schuetz, Wiley Carroll (deceased), Tony Kabonic, Major Boddicker, Ron McIntosh, and Tom Parr. A special thanks to Sami Jo Bybee of Frontier Photo for a great job with photo restoration and development and to Lesa Horrocks of Sunshine Secretarial for transcribing the transcript onto computer and disk, and for assistance in editing, and, finally, to Dale Burk of Stoneydale Press for his patience and assistance with final editing and photo enhancements.

Of the 14 magazines I gathered Bill's articles from, only one is still being published. That one is FUR-FISH-GAME and it published the majority of Bill's articles from 1935-1967. 1 used direct quotes and combination of quotes from some of Bill's old manuscripts, articles, and letters to other trappers as well as interviews and letters from others, to which I intermingled my own narrative. I have listed all the magazines and the articles and page numbers of Bill's writings that I have in my collection in THE AUTHOR chapter.

IDENTIFICATION OF OTHER PEOPLE MENTIONED THROUGHOUT THE BOOK AND THEIR RELATIONSHIP TO BILL NELSON

Edith Nelson(deceased): Bill's wife

Harry Batten: life-long friend and former trapping partner

Forrest Rider(deceased): life-long friend and former trapping partner

Marlene Rider: Forrest's daughter-in-law

Sonny Hootman: long-time friend and associate

Don Paul: friend and former student/trapping partner

Gus Gehlhar: friend and former student/trapping partner

Ruth Peterson: Edith's sister-in-law

Jack Harris: friend and former dealer

John Barbee: friend and former customer

Ron McIntosh: friend, former student and dealer

Fuller & Ruth(deceased) Laugeman: purchased Bill's lure business from Edith after his death

INTRODUCTION

It has been almost 50 years since I first heard of Bill Nelson through reading his articles and ads in FUR-FISH-GAME, THE NATIONAL TRAPPER'S DIGEST, AMERICAN WOODSMAN, AND TRAPPER'S LIFE magazines while growing up on a farm in southern Minnesota during the 1950s-1960s. Since we didn't have a TV, I spent a lot of evenings reading trapping books and magazines. There was something about his articles that captivated me more than ones from other outdoor writers of that time. He had a way with words that made you feel like you were right there with him on his ventures. It was very obvious he was knowledgeable about any subject he wrote about and his style of writing was also unique.

Sometime during the early 1960s, I bought his two trapping books and this changed my way of trapping from then on. The detailed descriptions and instructions were far more educational and informative than anything I had previously read. I then purchased some of his animal lures and the results from using them were astounding. Most memorable, I trapped 28 muskrats the first night using his methods and lures. That was more than I had previously trapped during an entire season on my school-day traplines.

During the early fall of 1969, I prepared to run my first all-season, full-time trapline for mink, muskrat, raccoon, and fox and I drove the 300-plus miles to Farmington, Iowa to buy my lures and bait for the season and to finally meet Bill Nelson in person. Upon arriving, I was impressed by the dark-haired, deep-voiced, slim man with a moustache and hair combed back that met me on the porch of their house. He introduced me to his wife, Edith, and we commenced visiting over a cup of pot-boiled coffee. It didn't take long to discover we had traveled through, and worked several areas, in common. When I told him where I lived in MN, he informed me he had spent a season trapping about 50 miles from there back in the 1930s and he recalled what large and well-marked skunks he had taken. More importantly, this area was where he had met

Edith. After listening to him relate some of his bounty-trapping experiences in northern MN, I informed him I had worked in, or driven through, some of those same areas while trapping and banding ducks for the MN Department of Natural Resources for the past 3 summers. We also discussed a fur company in MN I had worked part-time for while attending college, the year before. This company also had a branch office in IA that Bill was well familiar with. He was interested to hear how we skinned and put up large volumes of fur. While we visited, Bill would roll and smoke cigarettes, one after another. Edith would sometimes enter the conversations with stories of her own. Our visiting continued until noon and Edith prepared us a fine lunch. We continued to visit into the afternoon and I realized I should get my lures and bait and head back home. Instead, Bill invited me to spend the night and sleep on their couch in the living room, and I quickly accepted his offer. After dinner, we visited into the wee hours of the night. Early the next morning, I departed with my lures and bait and was completely overwhelmed and pumped-up by that first visit with him.

    We corresponded by mail a few times throughout that winter and into the spring of 1970. It was then he invited me to trap coyotes with him as a student/partner in his area during the upcoming fall and winter. Although coyote fur wasn't worth much, then, there was still a bounty paid on coyotes in IA. His proposition was that I would furnish all the traps, vehicle, and gas and he would furnish all the meals, lures and bait, country to trap, and of course, his extensive knowledge. He would arrange a room for me to rent at Bonaparte, a small town upriver from Farmington. My first impulse was to jump at the chance, but after contemplating buying the 200 #3 Victor double longspringed traps that he demanded, gas for the whole season, and other expenses, I did the math and convinced myself this would not be a profitable proposition for me, after splitting the bounty and fur money with him. Just the year before, I had completely outfitted myself with a mink and fox trapping outfit and I just couldn't justify or afford buying coyote traps, then. So, somewhat regretably, I wrote him back and passed on his offer. This was a decision I have regretted, ever since. Especially given the fact I would never get another chance. Bill did not resent me turning his offer down, and we continued to correspond and I visited him and Edith a few more times through 1972. It was ironic that I would move to MT the next year and began trapping coyotes a couple years after that.

    The last time I saw Bill Nelson was during the summer of 1972. It was almost sunset when I arrived at his house. Bill came out and leaned on my truck while we visited. He asked me about my plans for the upcoming trapping season. He told me he had been digging ginseng in MO that day and was very tired. He didn't look good, either. Little did I know he was sick and he didn't mention it. I took the hint and we bid farewell, which turned out to be our final one.

    I did not hear of his passing in March 1973 until a few months later, while I was living in MT. I was saddened to hear this and regretted not taking him up on his offer, more than ever.

    After his death, I began to collect articles he had written, old manuscripts, letters, photos, lure bottles, etc. Thirty years later, I realized that two generations of outdoorsmen had been born and were growing up without knowing who Bill Nelson was and what he had accomplished throughout his life and the contributions he had made. So, I decided to contact some of his former friends, trapping partners, and colleagues to learn more about him and then write a biography about him and detail his accomplishments and contributions. I already knew some of the aforementioned people, but I sought out several more and gathered even more valuable information that helped contribute to this book. Several of these people were getting up in the years, so I was fortunate to have visited with them while they were still alive. I did miss a few who had already passed on, unfortunately. My travels led me to Farmington and throughout IA, to northern MN, to MT, and to CA.

    I do not profess to have known Bill Nelson very well or that he even considered me to be his friend. In fact, the more I talked to others who really did know him better, the more I realized I knew very little about him. After talking to other people and comparing notes, I learned that several people knew "parts" of Bill, but no one individual knew "everything" about him. Only his wife, Edith, would know the most about him and she, too, was gone before I could interview her.

Although Bill Nelson was mostly known as a trapper, lure maker, and author, he was also an extraordinary wildcrafter, naturalist, student of nature, hunter, fisherman, and an all-around outdoorsman. Come with me, then, as we follow this Outdoorsman Extraordinaire from his boyhood in IA, to northern MN, to CA, and then back to IA, with a couple of side trips to MT and MN, and learn how he made his living from the outdoors, something most of us could only dream about.

Chapter 1

BOYHOOD AND THE EARLY YEARS

"I am most confident that I had very few ancestors that could have been called staid, everyday citizens. I am sure that if you took a close look into the branches of the old family tree, you would find them hanging heavy with bundles of beaver and wolf pelts; you would see dim forest trails, cold campfires along the way, and surely moccasined trappers bearing long rifles . . . I'll bet the only time their women folk saw them was on the rare occasions when they opened the cabin door, headed for the kitchen table, and started to tell about the wonderful country of furs, fish, and game that lay to the west or to the north over the next two mountain ranges. . . ."

Bill Nelson

William (Bill) Nelson was born August 23, 1908 in Keokuk, Iowa. He was adopted at an early age by Andrew and Hannah Moline Nelson, but he told Gus Gehlhar that his real last name was Riplinger. Bill was raised on a small farm south of Croton, IA, near the Des Moines River. His father died when he was quite young and his mother and grandmother pretty much raised him. He had no siblings. According to Harry Batten, Bill attended Johnson School, a small country school south of Croton, but he only attended through the 8th grade. Bill began his education from the great outdoors at an early age. He wrote, "*By the time I was 11, I spent far more of my daylight hours in the woods than I did at home. I played no games of cops and robbers. My 'play' was trapping and fishing. I hunted for relics of flint in the hills and along the creek beds, gathered wild berries and nuts, and spent endless hours watching nesting birds and fox dens along the creek bluff . . . .*"

Living close to a river, it was only natural that he would try his hand at fishing and he stated he had tried his first bankline fishing when he was 7 years old. He wrote, "*. . . I spent a lot of time on the river, learning the ways of the lazy rivers and the* *habits of the catfish. Even at that very early age, our table never wanted for catfish during the spring and summer months."* He caught his first sturgeon when he was a kid on a throw-line baited with worms and placed just below a gravel bar. While he was pulling in the line, he thought he had snagged a limb because there was no tugging on the line or movement, at all. Just before he reached the end of the line, the sturgeon lunged and splashed, and he landed the 9-pound *"uguly brute."*

Bill started his wildcrafting days at an early age, too. *"During my kid days, early spring and the first thaw meant the making of maple syrup. We had many large groves of giant hard maples on our farm and also on nearby farms. I would tap scores of maples and gather the syrup. A couple of giant black iron kettles answered as syrup pans for me. These were placed on stone supports and hardwood fires were built under them to boil the sap into syrup and maple sugar. I made several gallons each spring and sold some and kept the rest for home use."*

The coming of fall was one of Bill's favorite times of the year, even as a kid. *". . . Fall was when the trot lines were rolled up and the last mess of sizzling brown catfish were placed on the farm-house table. Then there would be the inventory of traps, the planning and*

Bill's farmsite south of Croton, IA. Buildings are all gone and property is now part of Shimek State Forest. (Sherm Blom photo)

prospecting for a new fur season. Visions of 'coon, mink, and fox hanging from the rafters in the old log barn . . . Soon then, the gabbling talk of the geese, and the watching for their long and uneven flight coming down from the north. Duck talk and whistling wings in the mornings, with the gray mists across the face of the river . . . It seems that the migrations of these winged wild-folk were always interwoven with trapping plans and dreams. On October nights, I used to stand under the big elms and listen to them. Now and then, the whistling scurry of wing beats as low-flying ducks rode the fall stern winds, and then the distant honk of a leader goose, a sound that soon blended with the ever-changing talks of the great flocks passing far overhead . . . With the coming of those first frosty nights, the heating stove in the front room of our farmhouse would pop and crackle with burning shell-bark hickory wood that threw off that wonderful old-time heating-stove warmth. When we would open the door to place more wood, a curl or two of fragrant hickory smoke would enter the room. There in front of the old stove, I would settle and surround myself with those great old trapper catalogs: TAYLOR, ROGERS, FUNSTEN, HILL, and many others. Think back to 1920, and I am sure many of you will remember the colorful trapping catalogs of that day. Every page was covered with eye-appeal pictures of animals, outdoor scenes, large cuts of traps, guns, and trapping equipment. Every catalog front cover was a masterpiece in presenting a huge trapped wolf struggling in the snow or a trapper's cabin tucked away in the green forest of the North, with the usual lazy plume of blue smoke drifting from the chimney. On the back covers appearing in color were cuts of lynx, wolf, otter, red fox, silver fox, marten, fisher, and all the lesser furbearers. I would turn the colorful pages and make new plans for my trapping season; and what dreams I would dream! Dreams of the future, of long snowy trails and the 'big bush,' of sable and wolf, and the grand panorama of wild mountains thrusting their peaks skyward in the far-back places. I am sure that I planned my life for the next 30 full years. I planned it and listened to the push and whisper of the first fall storms. I planned it while the night winds talked among the branches of the big elms near the old house . . . Dreams about the great outdoors and the following of long trails that lead to strange and exciting places. Among those dreams, there was one about the mighty Sierras and the trapping of glossy martens. . . ."

Bill's love of trapping was very evident from the beginning. "I am sure that the most prized possession I will ever have, or have had, was that old #1 Victor that my grandmother gave to me. That was a long time ago; so long that my hands barely fitted to the springs, much like they fit to a #4, now. That day, when I fondled that rusty old toe pincher, I am sure I began to form the foundation for the thousand-and-one trapper dreams that a so-young trapper must dream. The next 2 falls and winters, that old trap got some action, and more traps were added. My hands were stronger and those trap settings began to show clawed dirt and chewed brush and crudely-whittled fur forms begin to fill and those boyhood dreams continued to take new and interesting form." Like many of us, Bill's first attempts to trap furbearers were not successful, although he did catch some nontargets. ". . . I can remember how my mother placed a block of wood under the pans. At that time, I was only 7 years old and so all I had to do was to pull out the blocks and make my sets. Those rusty old Victors were my most cherished possessions. I would hike off, with traps across my shoulder, for the creek bottom on our farm. Along this creek, I would set my traps in any promising hole or den that I came across. These sets netted me cottontail rabbits and nothing else. However, I would be off at the crack of dawn to run my little trapline. I usually returned with from 2 to 4 rabbits jauntily displayed on the old harness-leather belt at my waist. This kind of trapping soon became too tame, though, and I started taking trapping lessons, from profusely-illustrated fur company catalogs and guide books."

Bill's mother, Hannah, with a tame deer on their farm (Bill Nelson photo)

Bill described the events leading up to his first furbearer catch. "During the fall of my 8th year on this old planet, my grandmother made me a present of an old, but good, #1-1/2 Victor. Once I got my hands on this man-sized trap, I had visions of a great fur season, ahead. Around the latter part of October, I could not hold out any longer, so with the old Victor in my hands, I headed for the creek. There was an old creek bed along this stream that was pretty well *grown up in yellow willows. Early fall rains had left 2-6" of water in this bed and I had been noticing the tracks of a huge 'coon along the muddy banks. At one pool that was a bit deeper than most of it, I had found 'coon tracks, galore. Those water-soaked willow leaves on the bottom no doubt was a hiding place for frogs and crawfish, so Mr. 'Coon was visiting it for his diet of frog legs and crawfish tails. To make a long story short, I spent a laboring 10 minutes getting the springs of that old trap smashed down and the trigger set. I had already covered the trap pan with bright, shiny tin foil. All I had left to do was fasten the trap and make the set. Luckily, there was a long pole handy that had been used at a water gap. To this, I fastened the trap chain with half a dozen new fencing staples. I placed the trap in a couple inches of water, covering all but the foil-wrapped pan. As I gave the set one last look, I could almost picture a big 'coon struggling there among the willows. I had high hopes.*

The following morning I managed by exercising unusual willpower, to keep away from the set and put out my six #1s in the usual dens and holes. One of them I set back in a meadow at a den that had long black and white hairs around the entrance. My book learning was beginning to take affect.

Well, the next morning I was on my way to tend traps, before breakfast. As I neared the pool in the creek bed, my heart was pounding like a trip hammer and I was putting on a little more speed with each step. Coming in sight of the set, I stopped short. The water in the pool was roiled and muddy, and the banks were dug up for several feet around the set. Freshly-chewed willows showed the path taken by the animal. Panting and stumbling, I started following the trail. Ahead of me, I could hear sounds of a struggle and the rattle of a trap chain. Then, I came in sight of my prize. There he stood, with his front foot firmly gripped in the jaws of the old Victor. What a picture he made! For a minute, he looked at me, then snarling and grunting, he resumed his struggles to free the drag wedged in the brush. Boy, how that old rascal could chew down the willows! I was afraid he would get loose if I clubbed him, so I took out for home yelling, 'coon!, 'coon!' and 'bring the gun,' at every jump.

My father met me with the rifle and we both hurried back to where my 'coon was waiting. When he saw the size of that 'coon, my father's eyes actually bulged. Quickly taking aim, he pulled the trigger on the little Remington and Mr. 'Coon rolled over, snarling and coughing in his death struggle. My father had to carry my watch for me while I marched proudly, alongside, with the rifle stuck back across my shoulder. That 'coon was a gaunt old ridge 'coon, and he weighed exactly 36 pounds. To this day, I have never seen his equal in size. Needless to say, that 'coon made me the proudest young trapper in the whole state of Iowa. It also started me along the trails of the far-back places that are followed by the pro trapper.

My next catch, strangely enough, was a mink. I had concealed a #1 at the entrance of a small hole in some rocks. I bled a trapped rabbit over the trap and on the rocks around the set. The very next morning, I found the trap pulled chains-length back in the hole. Taking a hold of the chain, I pulled out a snarling little female mink, I did another one of those yelling runs for dad and the rifle. . ."

". . . The next highlight in my trapping career was the taking of my first fox. I had set a #12 Oneida jump near a small pond in a back pasture for 'coon. I partly buried a chicken in some dry sand, concealing the trap on top. I clogged the trap with a section of oak saw the trap and clog were gone. On the other shore of the pond among a willow growth, I heard a splashing in the water and looked up, expecting to see a 'coon. Standing in shallow water and peeking at me through the willows, was a nice gray fox. What the devil he was standing there in the water for, I don't know . . . ." Bill later described catching his first red fox. ". . . How well I remember my first red fox, and the never-to-be-forgotten thrill of that catch. Along an old cattle trail that swung down over the brow of a ridge and through a stand of white oaks, I had concealed a #215X Triple Clutch trap. Now that big single-spring trap was my most prized possession at the time, and I was but a slip of a kid and the bulk of my traps were made up of old #1s. After spending a whole evening setting, springing, and admiring it, I had carefully treated it by boiling it in a solution of water and wild hay. From then on, it was handled only with a pair of clean leather gloves. The set was made where the roots of a giant oak jutted out, narrowing the trail. After concealing the trap and erasing all sign, I scented a gnarled surface root with just a dash of civet cat musk and went on my way. A neighboring farmer had told me of often seeing a fox along this ridge and once or twice, I had noticed tracks along the trail, so I had high hopes for my first actual fox set.

My first visit to this set resulted in a well-furred 'possum and a serious let-down in my hopes of a silky red, but just the same, the pelt helped swell the string of skunk, 'coon, 'possum, and civet cats hanging in the corncrib and I took extra care in resetting the trap. As I approached the set on my second trip around, I was in high spirits as the grain sack slung over my shoulder was already sagging with the weight of a pair of nice skunks. On sighting the set, I paused for a few seconds and stared in open-mouthed astonishment, then broke into a run. Believe it or not, there was a fine red fox lunging and jerking in the grip of that 215X. What a picture she made with her black-marked legs, silky red coat, and beautiful white-tipped tail. This female's fur was grayed with age and she had perhaps passed many a set more expertly-made than mine, but beginner's luck had spelled her doom.

Believe me, there was one mighty proud young trapper that day, cutting across the pastures for home. I was sweating and panting by the time I pulled up before the house to proudly display my first red fox. Those 2 skunks were completely disregarded . . . ."

Bill described how he used to run his school-day traplines. *". . . I used to start over my lines in the wee hours of the morning with a flashlight or carbide lamp. My line was laid out in the form of a loop. Other sets were run after school, still others, at night. The weekends were, of course, devoted to full-blown trapping activities . . . I usually finished it (the morning line) and trotted the remaining mile to the little country school, getting there just in time for the last bell. If I made a catch of striped 'woods kitties', I would miss a half day of school, so I always made sure I got plenty of perfume on me when I came up to a trapped skunk. If I located a 'possum in a hollow tree or snag, I promptly forgot all about school until that particular 'possum pelt was mine . . . Excitement ran high when a catch was made and soon the odor was high, too. The first season or two, I treated no skunk with care. I simply walked in and busted them with a club. After my third season with the traps, I proudly carried an old Remington single-shot rifle for killing trapped animals. This little 'pill slinger' helped a great deal in cutting down the odor of skunk around our farmhouse. Those southeast Iowa skunks brought a good price at that time. They bought more traps for* me, many of my clothes, and kept me in spending money. They meant a shiny, new flashlight for running my traps in the dark...."

During those early years, skunks were Bill's main catches. He trapped most of them at dens and later advanced to using baited sets at hollow-based trees and hollow logs and also natural-type cubby pens. Then he developed simple and effective bait sets that could be made almost anywhere by digging a small depression in the ground in front of a small backing, placing a bait into the depression, covering the bait with grass or other ground litter, concealing a trap in front of the bait, and pouring some lure on top of the concealed bait. He stated his fur catch began to increase after employing this simple set and it later became one of his better predator sets, with some modifications. Besides striped skunks, Bill also caught spotted skunks, or civet cats as they were commonly called, and 'possums at these types of sets. Regarding 'possums, he said, "I took hundreds of 'possums during my kid days and at that time, even this lowly critter brought a pretty fair price. I took a lot of them with dogs at night, too. I really burned the candle at both ends at that time...."

Living so close to the Des Moines River gave Bill an excellent setting for learning to trap muskrats and mink. He noted the river was much narrower in those days and both banks were lined with trees, willows, and shrubs. The banks were high and muddy and few sand bars were present. Natural foods for mink and muskrat were abundant. He noted there was a population of muskrats in the river at that time that fed on

Skunks & 'possums were his main catches on the school-day traplines. Here's a young Bill Nelson with a trapped 'possum. (Bill Nelson photo)

mussels. These flesh-eating muskrats were much larger than normal muskrats and were quite abundant. Like most beginning trappers, he used slide and den sets. Then, he advanced to apple or corn-on-a-stick sets and finally graduated to lured sets with eye appeal as described in his water trapping book.

Bill's first mink sets were simple sets made at the entrance of natural holes in the bluffs along and above the river and other creeks. Some were blind sets and others he baited with whole rabbit or muskrat carcasses, slit open, or chunks of fish, and covered them, lightly, with leaves or grass. The dry-hole sets would often yield skunks, civet cats, and 'possums and the water-hole sets sometimes yielded 'coons and muskrats, besides minks, and which were all welcomed. Bill noted, *"By the time I was 11, I was bringing in some really nice catches. Soon after that, I got the hang of mink trapping and then I was some trapper - at least in my own estimation."* During this time, he began keeping log books and notes on sets and lures and the resulting fur catches, a practice which he continued throughout his life.

Regarding 'coons, Bill remarked, *"During my early trapline days, the taking of a 'coon was rather rare. I worked quite hard one season during my early teens to make a catch of 17 'coons that seemed to be quite a 'coon catch at that time . . . The taking of a really giant old boar 'coon during those early days almost called for some sort of celebration, as I was taking far more mink than 'coon. Among other things, a big fat 'coon meant a 'coon roast supper with brown gravy, candied sweet potatoes, buttered apple pie, and all the trimmings."*

As mentioned, Bill trapped 'coons at hole sets for mink, but he also learned to use visible bait sets with live frogs, fish, and crayfish and then on to shelf and barricade sets which proved to be very effective.

Then came fox. *". . . A bit later on, the fox began to increase a bit and like all young trappers, I was severely bitten by the fox-fever bug. Many and fancy were my fox sets. I read everything in print and spent sleepless hours at night, dreaming up some super sets for the sly reds. I caught some foxes, too . . . I can well remember some of my kid-day fox takes. As I said before, fox were quite rare at that time, and I worked hard for the few I got. One day, I dreamed* up what I thought would be a killer set. I located dry cow pads in open pastures where I figured fox would travel and cross. Lifting the pad, I dug out a little basin and filled it with tainted muskrat flesh. Replacing the pad rather loosely over the bait, I made a double flat set with 2 traps, one trap carefully concealed on each side of the pad. On top of the pad, I smeared a rich mixture of fox gland material. Two feet up on a nearby bush, I placed a smear of my first fox call lure on a bit of rabbit fur. Well, believe it or not, I began to take fox. Not in great numbers, but I did take them and it gave me hope. The funny part about this set is the fact that it took me 20 years before I borrowed a bit from it and developed a simple and deadly set for both fox and coyote . . . However, I had my best luck in snow trapping and because I followed fox trails and let the fox teach me. Looking back to my kid-day fox trapping ventures, I remember few coyotes there at that time. Winters in IA during those days were colder than those we experience, today (1950). We had much more snow, too. I used to take a lot of mink each late season with snow sets. Some of those kid-day fox sets that I made in the snow were dandies."

Bill said he did not recall seeing otters during those days, but the old-timers, then, told him otters were very common and abundant, years before.

Since coyotes were so rare in that area during those days, Bill never expected to trap one while trapping fox. "I can well remember the time I first snapped steel on the foot of a coyote. I had made an open, or flat set, near a clump of dried grass on a large sand bar. The set had been made for red fox with a heavy smear of gland lure and a loud-smelling call lure, nearby. The trap was a #3 Blake and Lamb. It was a new set and on nearing it the next morning, I had the usual high hopes experienced by a trapper when approaching a new setting. When I looked out towards the bar, things did not look quite right, though nothing appeared torn up and there were no drag marks showing up or down the sandy creek bed. On crossing the creek, I saw the form of what I took to be a small police dog raise up from the dry vegetation back of the set. Not having anything but red fox associated with this set, I could only think that I had trapped a dog from a nearby farm. I just stopped and watched my 'police dog,' all the while figuring how to release it. About a second later, my 'dog' made a lunge and took out across the *sand on high gear, over the bank, and up the creek and out of sight. Only then, did I realize that my trapped 'dog' was actually a coyote. 'Wolf' to me at that time.*

Well, I spent 3 hours trying to find my coyote, and I was a very crestfallen young trapper that day. My first coyote lost, and coyotes were very rare animals in that section, those days. . . ."

It was a couple more years before Bill caught another coyote in another fox set and it too, escaped, leaving 2 toes in the trap. A few days later, he caught still another one in an old Diamond trap and it broke the chain and escaped, only to be found tangled in a fence and taken by some night hunters a week later, a couple of miles away.

It was not until he spent his first trapping season in northern MN that he would really get an education in trapping coyotes.

Bill summed up his early-day traplines. *"There is one thing, however, that I just cannot borrow from those early traplines. I cannot borrow that burning fever of preseason anticipation; that wonderful feeling I used to have that first day of the season when rusty traps were taken down and placed for the furry folk of hill and stream . . . Just nothing can quite bring the thrill of catches made along those early traplines, even if it was no more than a lowly skunk with its battle flag, erect."*

Bill ran his traplines on foot. He trapped with a few partners during those early years. Harry Batten trapped with Bill for 2 seasons and said they learned a lot from each other. Harry said Bill was a real hiker and could really "set a pace." They covered 15-20 miles per day on foot while running their traplines. Harry's brother also trapped with Bill for a season.

Sometime during his teens, Bill took up boxing and Harry used to train and spar with him. Bill was a scrapper in those days, and sometimes got into fist fights. Harry recalled one incident where Bill and another local man were fist-fighting in front of the Croton store and were moving up the street. Halfway through the fight, Bill called "time out" since his pants were loose and started to fall down. He asked the other man for his knife so he could punch a new hole into his belt. After fixing the belt, Bill tightened up his pants, returned the knife to his opponent, and they continued on with their fight. Harry never said who won, but we can assume Bill did.

Sometime during his early twenties, Bill moved to Davenport, IA and took a factory job at Nichols Wire Company. Harry said Bill was a handsome young man and quite stylish. He wore fancy clothes and shoes, a white Stetson hat, and even carried a white cane. During this period, Bill really got into boxing and fought in the Davenport and Chicago areas under the ring name of "Sailor Jones," according to Don Paul. He fought around 200 amateur fights before he turned pro as a middle-weight boxer and then went undefeated for 29 bouts. Bill told Don he wasn't that great a boxer, but all he wanted was an opening, and he could *"take out"* a man with one blow from either hand. Harry said, "Bill was a real slugger, and if he hit you, you were done." Unfortunately, Bill contracted scarlet fever and it weakened his heart, and he lost all his hair from the fever. The doctors told him to avoid strenuous physical activity, but Bill would not give up. He sent for a mail-order book on body building and slowly, but surely, worked himself into shape and back into the boxing ring. After 4 fights, Bill realized the fever had taken too much of a toll, and he hung up his gloves, *"before someone killed me."*

Bill's stylish manner and his success as a boxer brought him recognition and opportunities to meet many "beauties" during those days in Davenport. According to Harry, Bill did get married and they had a son. Bill told Don that his wife's interests were in the bright lights of the city and his were in the outdoors, so they divorced. Harry said Bill never did stay in touch with his son, after that. Bill then moved back to Croton to his beloved river and hills.

Chapter 2

NORTH TO MINNESOTA

While recovering from scarlet fever, Bill left his IA country in 1933 and moved into south-central MN at the age of 25. This was his first out-of-state venture, or "state-hopping," as it is now called. That summer, he honed his fishing skills on some of the lakes, there, while fishing for bass, northern pike, walleye, and panfish. As fall approached, he prepared to run a trapline for skunk, civet cat, mink, and weasel. During this time, he met Edith Peterson who was a bookkeeper at a hardware store in Clarks Grove. I do not know exactly when their courtship began, but they were not married until a couple years, later.

The next summer, Bill headed for northern MN to fish for the great muskies and prospect a trapline for the upcoming season. He spent time in several areas, but really liked the Big Fork area. His fishing skills became well known in the area, and he began to guide a few fishermen, especially for muskies. By fall, he had mapped out a trapline and located a base camp and spike camp to operate from. This was his first year of trapping in deep snow and extremely cold weather and he described it as follows.

The young fishing guide on a lake, somewhere in MN. (Bill Nelson photo)

"I believe it was Aristotle that said something about education or learning being accompanied by pain. During my first season in the north MN country, this proved to be true. My education in snow trapping for coyote, wolf, and 'cats was indeed well-laced with various types of pain. Unfortunately, I discarded some of the lessons that I had learned in the bitter school of experience and started out with some very fancy, tried some systems that surely had been invented by lads that had certainly never been on speaking terms with coyotes and true wolf; and especially under the type of warfare dictated by deep snows and the very deep sub-zero readings I had to buck. I made some sets that were indeed beautiful to behold. They were real masterpieces, but I did damn little fur taking and even less bounty collecting. I was testing some commercial dopes, too, that held less attraction in that severe cold than would common castor, liquid carrion, or pure skunk essence. I saw a lot of tracks in the snow, but none near those fancy sets and less-than-none on the trap-pan areas.

    I finally came back down to earth and made myself some good snow mounds, using my webs to construct them with. I used small lure posts at one end of them and also sunk some mighty stinking bait near the base of the lure post. I tore up the rim of those sets until it looked like a pair of bull moose had been battling there. I made those mounds and I made some other sets, and I started to cash in on both fur and bounty dollars." He had some advice. ". . . In snow trapping, you have two simple choices: either leave the set area appearing exactly as it was before making the set, or change things so completely that it actually excites the animal and makes it so curious that it seems to forget much of its natural caution . . . ." Bill described the set location where he trapped his first wolf as a point of land that jutted out into a small hidden lake. He made a snow-mound set and staked the trap solid. He trapped 3 coyotes at the set and they built him a "super mound" with plenty of eye and nose appeal. The wolf was catch number four and he caught another coyote and a bobcat, after that, proving it was an ideal set location and the value of animal odors at a set. After learning to trap coyotes and wolves in the snow, Bill concentrated on learning the ways of bobcats and how to trap them in snow, too. He spent endless hours tracking them through poplar groves, cedar bogs, around lakes and streams, and over the hills. With that knowledge and by experimenting with set locations, set types, and lures, he began to catch the 'cats. He described his first 'cat catch. "A snarling old she-devil of 23 pounds represented my first 'cat. She fell for a scratched-up stump set that was well-smeared with my very first bobcat lure, the #3 trap being well-concealed in rotten wood dust at the base of the *stump. . . That was one of my big trapping-thrill firsts."* He soon learned that eye and nose appeal at 'cat sets were very important to the success of trapping them.

Bill in front of his trapping cabin in northern MN with a small coyote he trapped. (Bill Nelson photo)

After surviving that first winter in the northern brush country of MN, Bill looked forward to the spring and summer seasons for fishing and prospecting more trapping areas. He continued to guide fishermen as a source of income. During that spring, the love bug bit him and he and Edith Peterson were married June 9, 1935 at Milaca, MN. He wasted no time in introducing her to the ways of an outdoorsman. She soon learned how to fish and enjoyed it as much as he did. When fall arrived, it was was time to prepare for trapping season. *"Very soon after Mrs. Bill and I were married, I hustled her off to a cold cabin resting along the shores of a MN lake. She selected the cabin, which happened to be the biggest and also the coldest and most drafty. She carried water from the lake, below, after cutting through the ice, and the water often froze in the bucket standing on the rough table at one end of the cabin. She learned to cook in that weathered old cabin and how to fire a big drum stove with great chunks of tamarack. We saw 55 below zero that winter and just a lot of -30 and -40. She learned to darn wool sox and I took some new lessons in snow trapping mink, wolf, coyote, and 'cat.*

The newly-wed "Mrs. Bill" with a northern pike she caught. (Bill Nelson photo)

21

Edith with a genuine birch-bark canoe, ready to go fishing on a river in northern MN. (Bill Nelson photo)

I had two line camps along a river to the north. Quite often I would be gone 5-6 days at a time. Upon my return, we would get that old stove, red hot, and we would spread a trapper feast on the table. We would celebrate and check over the furs thawing out on the cabin floor. Late at night, I would pile more wood wood into the stove and the smoke would curl out and fill the cabin with a woodsy fragrance. I could hear the poplars-frost pop, outside, and the deep rumble of ice buckling in the surrounding lakes and now and then, the wolf song, and it was all good." One can only imagine how Edith felt about being a new bride to this all-out trapper and spending her first winter with him in the bush.

After spending two years trapping in northern MN, Bill had some good advice for those who might consider following his footsteps. First, he recommended they read Raymond Thompson's book, THE WILDERNESS TRAPPER. Next, he told them to be prepared mentally, physically, and gear-wise. He advocated the best in clothing and equipment and stressed wool clothing to face the subzero temperatures they would encounter. He stressed one must know how to read a compass, and equally important, to believe it. As to traps, he recommended 200 #1-1/2s for minks, 'rats, and weasels; 60 #3s and 4s for

Edith with a nice big bobcat trapped by Bill in northern MN during their first winter, together. (Bill Nelson photo)

coyotes and wolves; and if fox were present, 60 #2s and 3s. If affordable, he recommended #14s and 48s for wolves. He said a good supply of operating money should be saved up for the entire season to last until some furs were sold. He warned trappers not to expect too much the first season, especially if coming in "cold." He also said extra snowshoes, clothing, and equipment should be left at the line cabins, as well as First Aid items, cold and flu medications, waterproof matches, flashlights, extra ammo, etc. And, he recommended starting to trap before the deep snows arrived. *"If a man is on location early enough in northern areas, much of his coyote, wolf, and bobcat work is well started before the snows come. In other words, he will have a mighty nice catch hung up before Old Man Winter complicates things for him . . . A wise north country trapper will have at least 30 full days of dirt work in before winter is at hand. And, those first 30 'magic days' are the days that decide how large a catch you will make for that season. Make no mistake about that."*

Chapter 3

SURVIVING THE DEPRESSION

After spending three years in MN, Bill and Edith returned to Farmington, IA during the summer of 1936. The Great Depression was on and work was very scarce. This did not bother Bill, and he went into the hills he knew so well and spent most of the summer digging ginseng and goldenseal roots which were dried and sold by the pound. He told me that he and Edith could afford to eat steaks when most people were trying to survive on salt pork and bacon. He also spent time fur prospecting and mapping out his traplines for the upcoming season. When fall arrived, he teamed up with a partner, Kennie, and they began trapping fox around the first of November. Bad weather set in, however, so they pulled their traps and waited for the general furbearer season to open, a short time away.

When it arrived, they spent long hours on foot, setting traps for mink, 'coon, fox, skunk, and 'possum. After a few days, it became obvious that skunks and 'possums were dominating their catches, along with a few civet cats. Mink were scarce, and he commented they were

Bill, left, and partner, Kennie, with a week's catch of furs taken on foot traplines during 1936 in the Great Depression.
(Bill Nelson photo)

just catching a few in the same areas where he had previously taken 20-36 in a season. For some unknown reason, muskrats were about gone and they only trapped 5 the entire season. They caught a few fox and even caught a couple coyotes which escaped their fox traps and which were still very rare in that area. Just as they started catching good numbers of 'coons, 'coon hunting season opened and that interfered with their trapping with 'coon hunters chasing 'coons at night with dogs. The hunters also cut down den trees, a practice which Bill despised.

Although he didn't reveal their total catch for the season, Bill did mention that mink brought $8-13, red fox $4-6, gray fox $1.75-2.75, skunk $1.75, and 'coon $6-7. This was very good money during the Depression and Bill summed it up as follows. *"For every dollar of fur we took, we received a hundred dollars worth of sport and added knowledge. And above all, we gained a priceless measure of health and happiness that is a trapper's, as he follows the long trails."*

Chapter 4

THE WILDCRAFTER

"The wildcrafter knows the clear tang of the early morning air and hears the first notes of the robin. He knows the sudden hush of the approaching night and hears the last lazy song of the brown thrasher among the plum thickets. He has the priviledge to walk through the shaded lanes of the trees and feel the soft blanket of the forest mulch beneath his feet; to glide by boat and canoe on the clear waters of lakes and ponds or along the winding course of lazy rivers; to spread his blanket on the warm soil and sleep, and to drift off to that dream-less sleep, counting the stars overhead and smelling the flowering things of the earth. That is the life of the wildcrafter and he gets far closer to nature than even the traplines or hunts can bring him."

Wildcrafting is harvesting nature's natural foods and products and selling them to supplement one's income. Wildcrafting includes mushroom gathering, hunting for Indian and other historical relics, panning for gold, commercial fishing, guiding, trapping turtles, gathering mussels for shells and pearls, picking wild berries, nuts, and fruits, distilling essential oils from plants, trees, and boughs, making maple or birch syrup, gathering medical roots and barks, gathering honey from wild bee hives, and gathering any other natural product that has marketable value. As mentioned in the first chapter, Bill began his wildcrafting days as a child because he thoroughly loved the outdoors and wanted to learn all he could from it and to earn spending money and contribute nature's bounty to the dinner table. During the Depression, his wildcrafting skills became an important part of his income and survival, especially given the fact he was married and had an extra responsibility. He wrote, *"During those bitter years of the Depression, the trained wildcrafter fared far better than average. Then, as now, his trade was anything but noble. It was indeed far more desirable than accepting public bounty or peddling bad hooch in country-town alleys. It was a living. In fact, a very good living and I know that for many, myself included, it was a good education. It brought us much closer to Mother Nature than we had ever been, before. It taught us a new respect and appreciation for the endless gifts that she offers to those that are eager to learn and willing to search. I think, too, that it made better men out of us. It taught us to think, and it taught us to look and see the wonders that were created for us. Certainly, it brought us bread, meat, and clothing."*

ROOT DIGGING

The dried roots from several plants are used in pharmaceutical preparations and medicines, even today. Years ago, they were commonly called "medical roots." Medical roots included ginseng, goldenseal, Virginia and Seneca snakeroot, wild ginger, mayapple, and bloodroot, just to name a few. Bill mostly dug ginseng and goldenseal roots, since they were the most abundant in his area and the most profitable. Although one could dig "'seng" and "'seal" almost anytime during the summer, he preferred September and early October to the other months, because the plants were a little easier to spot and the temperatures were much more pleasant to work in. Also, mosquitoes were less troublesome.

Bill hunted for goldenseal plants in shaded areas along the flats adjacent to ditches and creeks, along the slopes and at the bases of hills and bluffs among second-growth oak, hazel brush, basswood, butternut, and maple trees. He stressed that heavily- pastured areas would not contain many goldenseal plants because livestock would eat and trample them and the resulting sod would also smother them. He hunted for plants by walking slow and careful grids, back-and-forth, across areas he suspected plants to be growing.

He stated that ginseng plants needed plenty of natural shade and grew best in heavy clay soil that was well-mulched with leaves. Unlike 'seal, it was seldom found in heavy oak timber. Rather, it favored maple, basswood, butternut, ash, and similar trees. He sometimes found it growing around clumps of hazel, gooseberry bushes, bloodroot, wild ginger, and other plants. When hunting new country, he recommended looking for 'seng on the north and west slopes of hills and bluffs, strips of unpastured land, old fence rows, heads of draws, and the flats next to bluffs along creeks and rivers. He noted that 'seng was much harder to locate and harder to see than 'seal. He admitted he had often walked right by patches, only to find them, later. Hunting for 'seng was easier after they formed their red berries, he said. After locating a plant or group of plants, he would mark the location and then slowly walk in expanding circles to locate any more plants. Once located, he carefully dug out the plant and roots with a screwdriver and with his fingers, as not to damage the precious roots. Since 'seng takes at least 7-10 years to grow back, he "farmed" plants back into the patch by replanting seeds, young plants that weren't harvestable, and root cuttings. He would leave those patches alone for as long as it took to grow plants to maturity. He was adamant about that practice and scorned other root diggers who did not replant after harvesting. This was just a good conservation practice and insured a future income, years later.

Bill with some freshly-dug goldenseal plants.
(Bill Nelson photo)

Although most root-diggers were very secretive about their operations, locations of plants, and prices they received for their roots, Bill wrote that he had dug 16 pounds of 'seal roots (dried) in 5 trips and another 10 pounds in 3 trips. He once dug 56 pounds of raw roots in 2 days. He would usually start hunting for plants early in the morning and sometimes would not find a patch until noon, or after.

Sometimes he brought Edith with to help him dig roots and to fan mosquitoes and gnats away from him while he dug. It was not all that pleasant. He wrote, *"We spent some rugged days in the timber during the heat of August and early September* that would have folded many a man. Some of those spots were along deep canyons where not a single breath of breeze broke the humid heat. Mosquitoes would settle down on me in clouds in spite of the dope-smeared face and clothing. My wife used to make up sweeps from the stems and leaves of plants. While I dug, she would fan away the blasted bugs. All in all, we had our share of hardships." Poisonous snakes were a real danger to him as he dug roots. They were often coiled up under plants and he could not see them until he was right over them. Rattlesnakes would buzz a warning, but copperheads did not. Sonny Hootman said that Bill was bitten in the arm by a copperhead, once, and his arm swelled up and turned an ugly black-and-blue color. He recovered, though, and didn't lose his arm. Even after a day of hardships, Bill would describe the good things they enjoyed after returning from a long hot day in the field. "Upon our return home after a rugged day, we would bathe and rub down with alcohol. We would have a feast that often included luscious wild berries gathered enroute to the root country. Then, after a rest, came the best part of the day. We would wash the roots, drain them, and then spread them out to dry. The smell of drying roots is not to be forgotten."

Edith spreading out 56 pounds of golden' seal roots to dry that Bill dug in 2 days
(Bill Nelson photo)

Bill with some dried 'seng and 'seal roots ready to ship to market.
(Bill Nelson photo)

After the roots had dried, they were packed in clean burlap bags and then boxed for shipment. During those Depression years, Bill said he could make $2-5 per day digging 'seal and some days as much as $6-12. 'Seng roots brought $7-8.50 per pound, too, which was very good money, then.

It was a shame that Bill couldn't have lived a few more years to see 'seal bring over $40 per pound and 'seng over $300. Some of the many patches he harvested and nurtured in the hills around Farmington for so many years have probably been destroyed by land clearing and development, but others have probably not been harvested since he died and stand tall, as a tribute to him.

FLOWER GARDENING

Bill also supplemented his income during the summer by raising flowers and sell them, locally, for weddings, funerals, anniversaries and other social events. He specialized in raising gladiolas. Sonny Hootman said that several people around Farmington would let Bill use spaces in their lawns or gardens to grow flowers, both to help him out and to enhance the beauty of their own places. Bill would cut and prepare the floral bouquets and deliver them to their destinations in his car. He was "in demand" and well known for his floral arrangements.

SHELLING

Years ago, fresh-water clams, or mussels as they were commonly called, were commercially harvested for their shells which were cut and made into buttons for clothing. Rare pearls were sometimes found within the shells, and they were greatly sought after. Bill also utilized the meats from mussels for food and also for some of his animal lures and catfish baits.

Muscatine, Iowa was the "capitol" of the button factories, but other factories were located at Washington and Davenport, IA, Andalusia, IL, Louisiana, MO, and several other "river towns" in that region.

"Shelling," or gathering mussels by hand from river bottoms, was hard work and done mostly during the late-summer months after the waters had reached their low. It was hot and humid, then, and the mosquitoes were out in full force. Severe thunderstorms, and even tornadoes, were sometimes a threat. Bill's method of gathering mussels was to strip down to short swimming trunks and sneakers, and with gloved hands, he would search and feel for mussels on the river bottom. He stated that if gloves were not worn, one's hands would become bloody-raw after a few hours of digging. He used a little flat-bottomed boat and an 8-foot float to haul the mussels to shore. As he dug the mussels one at a time, he would toss them into the float until it was full and then pull it over to the boat and empty the mussels into it. He usually had the boat filled by noon, so would head for shore to unload and eat lunch with Edith. After lunch, he would resume digging and fill another boat-load, by dark. On shore, Edith would cook the mussels in a big kettle over an open fire until the shells could be pryed open. She would then open each one, remove the meat, and check for pearls or lesser slugs and baroques. Sometimes, she could not keep up with Bill, so they hired a couple kids from town to help her clean and sort shells. They had several "shell camps" along the Des Moines River where they would stay for days and weeks on end during the

The Des Moines River on a hot, hazy, and muggy day where Bill dug mussels by hand. (Bill Nelson photo)

One of the Nelson's shell camps and a few tons of shells all sorted and ready for trucks to haul them to a button factory. (Bill Nelson photo)

shelling season, clear into fall. They usually slept out in the open since the nights were so hot and humid, but they had a tent-fly and tent set up for when it rained.

Bill described how a day began at their shell camp. "*Work began in the mornings before sun-up. There was just a pale blush of light to the east when we stirred and dug bare feet in the white sand at bed side. Soon, a cheery campfire pushed back the shadows and threw our camp into bold relief . . . An old oil stove served as a cook range and Edith quickly had the 3 burners busy with sizzling bacon and eggs and that lovely old camp pot filled with fragrant frown coffee . . . It was still dark on the river when I started out.*"

It was usually after dark by the time Bill returned to camp with the second boat-load of mussels and he was more than ready for the big dinner that Edith had prepared. No time was wasted in bedding down for the night. "*After the evening meal, I would stretch out on the warm sand and watch the river and listen to the lazy, soft sounds of the moving water. It is then that a thousand and one other sounds stir to life. First, the frogs along the water's edge, then the tree frogs, and finally, the countless insects . . . we could ask for no better roof than the great arch of sky above us and the spreading branches of giant cottonwoods and sycamores. This allowed us to drift off to sleep listening to the night sounds and watch the countless stars overhead and the cloud boats scuddle across the face of a great summer moon.*"

Bill made more money on the shells when he pregraded them into separate piles. Normally, the "river-run" grade consisting of three-ribs, blue points, monkey faces, and pimple backs sold for $40 per ton. The next better "mucket" grade consisting of pocket books, black sands, buckhorns, and maple leafs brought $50 per ton. Finally, the best grade shells called "yellow sands", sold for $90 per ton. He said the highest prices he had received on the 3 grades were $65, $100, and $160, respectively.

We'll never know how many tons of mussel shells Bill gathered during those years, but he mentioned in one of his articles, "*. . . That summer, the big trucks came three times to haul our shells away . . . .*" Harry Batten said that some of the piles of shells Bill piled up were as tall as some houses.

Bill summed up the life he and Edith spent at their summer shell camps. *"You get tough in a shell camp. You become hard as nails and burned by the wind and sun to a deep copper. You feel good after taking health by the hand for a full summer of river life. And, you hate like the devil to leave the river when the time comes to go home."* Edith once said, "Gosh, but it is going to be hard to sleep in a bed, again."

Many years later, Bill lamented the demise of the Des Moines River and the end of the era of shelling and pearling. *"Since that time, man's ax and saw, his plow, his cultivator, and his sewage disposal has about ruined what was once a very fine shell, fish, and fur river. The unprotected banks have crumbled and washed away. The river has widened and flattened out to sand bars and mud flats. The fields have sluffed their top soil into it and the vegetation is gone. Even the mussel life is about gone because the river is now shallow, silty, and fouled with sewage that a slow-moving stream cannot sluff off."*

Bill with his collection of various types of mussels. (Bill Nelson photo)

PEARLING

Bill referred to pearls as *"fresh-water gems."* He wrote several articles on the origin and formation of pearls, the types and classification of them, and brief instructions on cleaning and preparing them for market. He described how pearls had been highly-valued throughout the ages for their beauty and so-called mystical powers. He noted the fact they are produced by a living process from one of the lowest forms of life which, in itself, is miraculous. He scorned the appearance of cultured pearls that were beginning to appear on the market at that time, as well as imported pearls from foreign countries, especially the Orient. He considered those pearls as vastly inferior to American ones.

Bill described how pearls are formed by a parasite that enters the body of the mussel and attaches itself to the thin tissue-like mantle. This causes an irritation to the mussel and it begins to coat the irritating object with thin, concentric layers of nacre that subjects the irritation to a slow rolling movement. If this process continues without interruption, a quality pearl may be formed. If something goes wrong in the rolling process, or the irritation becomes loosened and moves from the mantle to the face of the inner shell, they may become deformed. Ideally, pearls are found near the posterior lip of the shell and mantle. Factors such as mineral content of the water, size of the parasite, the extent of the irritation, the species of mussel, and the ability of the individual mussel to produce nacre also play important roles in the formation of pearls. In some rare cases, pearls are shed by the mussel and found laying along the shore. He thought the whole body of the mussel was shed from the shell in those cases, and the pearl appeared after the body meat had decomposed and disappeared. He noted that in low water and hot temperatures, many mussels died and were left to decompose above water line.

In classifying pearls, Bill said "pear" pearls or "drop" pearls were the most valuable and were almost perfectly round and symmetrical. "High buttons" were pearls with slightly flattened edges and "low buttons" were those with pronounced flattening and low domes. Pearls flattened on both sides were called "biscuit" pearls. Pearls appearing like barrels or eggs were thus named. "Drop" pearls were the rarest type and most sought after, he said.

Bill noted there were over 600 species and subspecies of fresh-water mussels, with 36 of them being the most important to the shelling and button industry. Some species were more apt to become infected with parasites than others and therefore, were more important to the pearl gatherers.

Sometimes, very unusual and irregular-shaped pearls were found and they were called "rose buds," "strawberries," or "turtlebacks." Very small pearls were called "seeds."

Parasites sometimes infected the sides of the mussel's body, the flesh near the abductor muscles, along the shell hinge, and even the teeth. The resulting pieces were irregular in shape and size and lacked the true lustre of regular pearls. Those kinds were classified as "baroques." Long, smooth pieces formed along the shell hinges were called "spikeds," "hinges," or "tooths." Larger pieces were called "slugs" or "nuggets."

Most high-grade pearls were a lustrous, semi-translucent white. Other colors such as gold, pink, blue, silver-gray, red, and green also appeared as shades within the white.

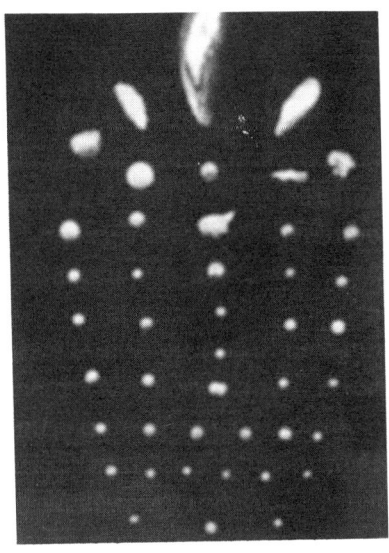

Bill's collection of pearls, baroques, and seed pearls.
Top row, left to right: blue-white turtle-back pearl, white baroque, bronze baroque, white baroque. Second row, left to right: white low-button pearl, lavender high-button pearl, white wing baroque, pink rosebud pearl. Rest are white-ball pearls, baroques, and seed pears. (Bill Nelson photo)

Pearls were graded according to shape and size and weighed by the grain. In those days, Bill said good pearls could bring from $5-1,000 each. Smaller seed pearls brought $10-50 per ounce, nuggets and spikes brought $5-25 per ounce, and slugs started at $3 per ounce. He said good pearls were sold to markets in Europe, India, and Persia.

Bill stated pearls were composed of over 90% carbonate of lime, 6% organic matter, and the rest, water. Good gem pearls would weigh 30-100 grains and be of the proper color of white or delicate pink and be absolutely symmetrical and flawless. Bill recalled some individual gem pearls that had been sold over the years for high prices of $4,500 to over $200,000. The latter price was a gem pearl sold to Queen Ann of Holland. One local harvester he knew sold two pearls for $1,200.

As to the success of finding pearls, Bill stated it as such. "It all depends upon how hard you work at this shell and pearl-hunting game, how much you have studied and learned about mussels and their habits, fish host and mussel relationship, parasites and parasite waters, and upon how well you know your river. And . . . it also depends on how the cards fall for you, when you sit in at this great river gamble."

As with most wildcrafting activities, Bill warned the wise shell and/or pearl harvester to keep quiet about his activities and success to prevent publicity and the resulting "crazes" that could occur and cause massive harvests and waste. He did, however, list some of the noted rivers that had gained the reputation as "pearl streams." They included the whole Mississippi River system, Black, White, Ohio, Illinois, Rock, Scioto, Sugar, Cumberland, and the Tennessee Rivers. He was careful not to mention his "own" river by name, but it was, of course, the Des Moines, and he said he had as much faith in it as the reputation rivers, he listed.

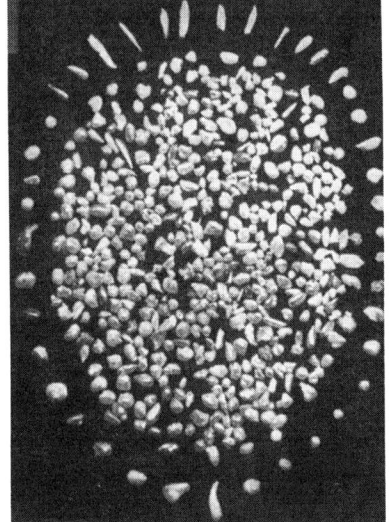

Bill's collection of slugs, nuggets, and baroques. (Bill Nelson photo)

Bill mentioned the importance of saving the lower-grade materials. He said he had paid for a season's shelling expenses through the sales of slugs, alone, thereby leaving the more valuable pearls and baroques for profit. One summer, he and Edith gathered over one pound of fine slugs, nuggets, and baroques and 2-3 fair pearls which provided them with a nice bonus to the tons of shells they sold. Bill also bought pearl items from other harvesters or brokered for them through his market connections.

As shelling and pearling became a thing of the past due to buttons being made from plastic and commercial harvesting of mussels heavily-regulated or curtailed, Bill lamented the passing of an era and the decline in overall wildcrafting. "*I dislike seeing any branch of wildcrafting become dormant and neglected. One need not be a professional to enjoy pearl hunting, shelling, root and herb gathering, turtle hunting, fishing, gem hunting, etc. that so many of us used to make a good living with. A few days or weeks spent along rivers and over the wooded hills is a darn good investment in health and the almost lost art of enjoying life and the wonderful things that Mother Nature has so wisely and generously provided for us.*"

```
******SHELLERS****PEARL HUNTERS******
I have the finest export and domestic
market contacts in the nation for all
pearl material. Have been handling
small and large lots for many years,
and can obtain the highest possible
prices for you. Market on average run
small slugs is slow, but is very good
on large, smooth slugs. Good sized
ball and button pearls moving very
well at good prices. Also rose-buds,
strawberry and turtle-back baroques.
I am a river man of experience in this
game, and, I assure you, know my way
around. No sales made until shipper
okays price. Be sure to insure ship-
ments.

BILL NELSON,              FARMINGTON, IOWA
```

Bill's ad for brokering other's pearl materials.

In one of Bill's last articles, if not the last, he summarized his and Edith's wildcrafting seasons. "*. . . Early in May, we were after those tasty mushrooms, or wood morels, native to our shaded timber gullies . . . I begin to dig roots later in May and continued through June and into early July. About that time, the river stage was low enough to permit good shelling. The wife and I would put away the root tools and the old root packs. We would dig out the tent and camping equipment and head for our river. There, we would pitch our tent near good shoal waters and spend the rest of the summer and early fall digging shells and pearling. What a great and wonderful life that was! We raised several large gardens and filled the old cellar to over-flowing with canned foods. We stored beans and both Irish and sweet potatoes. We gathered wood morels and buckets of wild berries. I made rich wine from frosted wild grapes. We faced heat and storms, ticks and mosquitoes, thorns and snakes after the 'seal root and the stately ginseng. We lived on the river and piled up mounds of saleable mussel shells and tucked away little jars of brilliant slugs and baroques and a few cotton-wrapped pearls. We fried skillets of golden-browned catfish and ate wild honey and melons from our gardens. We watched and listened to the wild birds of forests and fields. We watched the flowering things of the* *earth that take life each new spring and watched the magic of color come to autumn leaves. Certainly, we walked hand-in-hand with nature. We were as hard as nails and brown as autumn berries, and we lived and enjoyed life to the utmost. My only regret is that I am not still doing it."*

Chapter 5

WEST TO CALIFORNIA

After trapping in Iowa during the 1937-38 season, Bill became discouraged from losing fur and traps to *"sneaking"* thieves. He considered going back to MN or some other northern state, again, and had 2 prospective partners willing to work with him. But after careful consideration and feeling the urge to live out another of his boyhood dreams of trapping in the mountains of the West, he chose instead to team up with a man from MO he had never met, personally, but had corresponded with, by letters. This man claimed to already be a good coyote and bobcat trapper as well as having water-trapping experience. Like Bill, he was interested in trying his hand at trapping in the West. So, on September 18, 1938, Bill said goodbye to Edith on what was to be a 5-month venture, and he headed south into MO to pick up his new partner, whom he didn't identify. The trip started out badly as he had a tire blow out and ignition trouble near Jefferson City. After repairing them, he continued south around Lake of the Ozarks and to his *"pard's"* farm near the White River, about 9 miles from the AR border. After spending a few days getting their traps, tent camp, and other equipment ready and packed, they left early on the morning of the 23rd and headed west on Route 66 through a corner of KS and into OK, through Tulsa and OK City, into the TX panhandle through Amarillo, into NM, through Albuquerque and Gallup, into AZ through Flagstaff and Kingman. They considered visiting Boulder Dam and the Grand Canyon, but decided not to and continued west across the CO River into Needles, CA, through Daggett, Barstow, Bakersfield, and Fresno. They camped out, nights, and did their own cooking, to save on expenses. By October 4th, they felt they had reached "the place" as they viewed the Coast Range of western CA and entered Mendocino County. That day, they made a 12-mile prospect trip for 2 hours and Bill remarked how impressed he was with the size and beauty of the redwood trees, there.

TRAPPING ON FOOT IN THE COASTAL RANGES

After locating a base to operate from and unloading their traps and gear, they began to prospect in earnest on October 16th. It didn't take long for Bill to size up his new pardner and he said, "*I am afraid my Pard is not a true trapper and that his experience is very limited, indeed. Perhaps he is willing enough to make up for it, though.*" After surveying the area, they decided 'coons would be their main target, followed by minks, gray foxes, bobcats, and whatever skunks, ringtails, civet cats, etc. they could pick up. Their traplines were run on foot, and each of them ran separate lines. By November 9th they were catching fur. On November 20th, they bundled up their first batch of furs consisting of mink, skunk, skunk, civet cat, ringtail, bobcat, 'coon, and gray fox and shipped them to Seattle so they could receive some operating money. Bill noted he had caught his first ringtail on this trapline and admired its beauty and interesting colors. Heavy rains forced them to quit trapping until December 9th. Soon afterwards, he caught a 14-1/2 pound 'coon which was the biggest one they had taken, thus far.

Bill noted they had trapped two distinct subspecies of bobcats along their lines and he complained the Bureau of Biological Survey had destroyed many coyotes, bobcats, and gray foxes in that region by their extermination programs with the use of poisons.

During this time, Bill met a local trapper, Jack Foster, who would later trap with him and also work, together, on other ventures.

By January 17, 1939, Bill wrote they had skinned 55 'coons and lost another 15 to pull-outs. On January 23rd, they shipped their 5th batch of furs to Seattle. Also on that day, Bill noted he had trapped the palest gray fox he had ever seen. It was much different than eastern and midwestern species he had trapped, with longer ears and lacking black-marked legs. He also spent considerable time trying to find the rare Humboldt marten which he was sure ranged in those mountains. He finally found some, and added a few of them to the fur catch.

Bill had made two cougar sets along some rough rim rocks near the head of a stream. Upon checking the sets, he discovered he had caught a cougar in one of the sets, but it had broken the tie-wire on the #4 trap and escaped. He returned to camp and got Jack Foster and his dogs to go with him the next day to see if they could track down the cougar, but they never did find it.

By February 2nd, Bill commented the rains and snows had set in to stay and he suspected his pard would soon journey back to MO. By that time, they had skinned 80 'coons and 24 bobcats.

Bill continued to trap by himself until February 17th and then spent a couple weeks surveying the surrounding areas of Covelo, the Lake Mountain country, and the Yolla Bolly primitive area to the northeast.

After the short prospect trip, Bill and Jack Foster drove to the Pacific coast for a few days of fishing and r&r. After that, they sought employment in a logging camp as "fallers". Falling timber involved a 2-man crosscut saw and ax; no chain saws in those days. Bill told Don Paul they were paid by the number of trees they fell, not by the foot or an hourly wage. He also related an off-duty incident that almost cost them their lives. He and Jack had gone to town on a Saturday night to *"loosen up"* and have a few drinks. The bar was filled with Indians and many of them were drunk. When he and Jack decided to leave, several Indians followed them out and began fighting with, and knocking them down. Bill finally made it back to the car where he had a pistol to fend off their

Bill's first partner in CA (unidentified) and part of their catch that included 'coon, skunk, civet cat, mink, ringtail, bobcat, and bear. Note the 4 very rare Humboldt martens in the upper right corner. (Bill Nelson photo)

attackers and he and Jack escaped with some bumps, cuts, and bruises. But at least they were still alive. What had started out to be a 5-month trapping venture in 1938 extended into the next fall of 1939 when Bill teamed up with Jack Foster and they trapped farther north into Trinity and Humboldt Counties as well as a small part of Del Norte County and later into the Coastal Range. Again, they trapped on foot and Bill told Don Paul they packed all their traps, equipment, dried food, etc. in on their backs and slept out in the open or under crude shelters in sleeping bags until they could build some crude cabins. He remarked this was the period he really became a successful trapper and outdoorsman. He had to; it was simply succeed or starve. Again, they trapped the same species as before, and Bill added otters to the species he had trapped. He mentioned catching a 25-pound otter that stretched 65" on the board. He and Jack both placed a few bear and cougar sets and caught several of each. Bill really wanted some good photos of trapped bears in a bad mood, popping their teeth and tossing their heads back and forth. But every time they caught one in a #14 trap set for cougars, it was barely held by its toes or it was thrashing around so much they were afraid it would pull out of the trap, so it was not safe or feasible to get good photos. Finally, he had enough and said, *"To hell with bear pictures!"*

Bill was surprised to hear from Jack Foster that wolverines were present in CA and Jack had actually seen mounted specimens near Tulare. This unique subspecies of wolverine was found mostly in the Yosemite area of the Sierras at that time.

In mid-December, they moved into the Coast Range and trapped there until mid-March of 1940. By mid-February Bill mentioned they had trapped over 130 skunks and 40 civet cats on their foot traplines.

Some furs trapped by Bill and Jack Foster that include coyote, bobcat, gray fox, civet cat, skunk, 'coon, ringtail, mink, and otter. (Bill Nelson photo)

After trapping season, they did a little gold panning and Bill remarked they had *"fair success."* After being gone from Edith for over 18 months, Bill returned to IA and Jack Foster went on to be a noted state trapper in CA.

Bill spent the rest of 1940 in IA and into the spring of 1941. His boyhood dream of trapping martens in the Sierras kept tugging at him, however, so later in the summer, he loaded up Edith and they headed back to the Humboldt County country for one more season after the rare Humboldt marten and also to hone his bobcat trapping skills and test more lures on them. He mentioned the cut-over redwood areas with a lot of brush were exceptionally good 'cat habitat, there. Although he did not elaborate on that season nor what his total catch was, he did say he had trapped a number of Humboldt marten and had received as high as $24.50 for some of them. He also mentioned catching a *"good number"* of 'cats.

WORKING FOR THE U.S. FOREST SERVICE

Sometime during the spring of 1942, Bill and Edith moved to the little town of Downieville in the northern area of the Sierra Nevada mountains. Bill was hired by the U.S. Forest Service as a firefighter, or "runner," as they were commonly called, since they "ran" all over the state fighting fires throughout the summer fire season. It didn't take long for Bill to decide he wanted to get a permanent position with the FS. He was in his 30s and had a wife to support and it seemed to be a good profession for him to enter. He told Don Paul that he went to public libraries and read and learned all he could about forest management, tree classification, fire-fighting, etc. so he could advance his position. His hard work and superior performance paid off, and he was promoted to a crew foreman. The next year (1943), he was promoted to District Fire Dispatcher and by fall, he was promoted to Assistant Fire Control Officer for the whole state of CA. Quite an accomplishment in such a short period of time for a guy who just had an eighth-grade education. That sure said something for his desire to exceed and willingness to stop at nothing to achieve his goals. He described some of his duties as fire control prevention, personnel training, improvement work supervisor, office management, recreational planning, issuing special-use permits, and timber management. He commented the fire season of 1945 was a tough one and he had spent a good portion of the summer in southern CA fighting a big fire on the Cleveland Forest.

Working for the FS allowed Bill to accumulate annual leave, something he had never experienced, before. Not surprisingly, he usually saved up all his earned leave until winter, so he could run short prospect traplines and learn the country and how to trap in new and challenging conditions, which he did during 1942-1944. Since fire prevention and timber management involved aerial surveys, he quickly learned that he could use those flights to aerially-prospect future traplines and learn how the ridge systems connected, locations of lakes, streams, and basins and other land features that would help him to map and run his traplines.

Sometime during 1945, Bill must have had enough of the high stress, heavy demands, office setting, and paperwork of his administrative position with the FS, and although he didn't elaborate, he did write a vague explanation. "... *Two weeks later, a lot of decisions had been made by me and later, still, they were speeded by existing conditions that no breather of free and clean air could tolerate.*" So ended his brief career with the FS and this was one of the last jobs he ever had, working for someone else.

During his 3 years with the FS, Bill learned to ski while doing snow surveys during the winter months. He commented he had skied over 1,000 miles during that period.

VACATION PROSPECT LINES

As mentioned, Bill usually saved up his annual leave for the winter months so he could fulfill that boyhood dream of trapping marten in the Sierras. He called them prospect lines, since he only had 2-3 weeks to trap, which was not enough time to run the full-blown traplines he was accustomed to. He described one of these prospect lines for a week, or so, where he took Edith with him since a busy fire season had kept him away from her for long periods of time. They and their 2 dogs left early in the morning on skis and traveled up to their base camp. This was Edith's first time on the marten line and she was very enthusiastic about it all. After 2 hours of traveling, they stopped for a tea and snack break, and then took their time the rest of the way, as not to tire her too much. They arrived at the cabin by late afternoon only to find it almost covered by snow. Bill had to dig down six feet to the door with a shovel he had previously cached high in a nearby tree and he also made steps down to it. That done, he got a fire going in the wood stove while she prepared a big pot of coffee and supper. After stuffing themselves and drinking 2 pots of coffee, they collapsed into bed into a deep sleep.

Only the top of the roof of the cabin was showing when they arrived. (Bill Nelson photo)

They slept in the next morning and after a big breakfast, he started setting out his trapline while she stayed in camp and *"got things in order."* Bill made a few coyote and 'cat sets near camp as he noticed some sign, and then headed for marten country. He made his first group of marten sets a mile from camp at the junction of 2 ridges above an alpine basin. He continued extending his lines along the main divides

Edith standing in front of the door after Bill had to shovel through 6' of snow and build steps down to it. (Photo courtesy of Marlene Rider)

and basins and didn't return to camp until almost dark. He wrote, "*Edith had a meal fit for a king waiting for me and to say that I ate enough for 3 men that night would be at best, an understatement. Just for good measure, I downed an extra pot of rich, brown coffee, myself.*"

The next morning, Edith accompanied him to set out another line. It was a cold, but windless day. As they started out, they heard a train whistle, miles to the north, from the railroad along the Feather River. By noon, they reached the summit and stopped to build a fire for tea and lunch. Bill then began setting traps along the main divide ridge, alpine lakes, and at the rims of slides. By late afternoon, he had made over 20 new sets and they headed for the cabin. After 20 miles of ski travel that day, Edith was totally wore out, so when they arrived at camp, Bill graciously cooked supper while she rested her aching muscles.

Stiff and sore as she was the next morning, Edith insisted on going out to check those traps. As luck would have it, the first marten he trapped was still alive, and Edith was thrilled by the sight. By the end of the day, 2 more martens were added to his pack. After returning to the cabin, Edith admired the 3 glossy martens and Bill said she began to comment about the prospects of her getting a marten scarf, someday.

Two days later, a big storm hit and made traveling very dangerous, so Bill traveled, alone, while checking his traplines. He picked up a few coyotes and 'cats and also a big buck marten, the largest of the season.

By the time the storm subsided, Bill's vacation time was about used up, so he pulled up his traps, and Edith accompanied him the last day. "*. . . That last day was our best, partly because we knew it was our last. We enjoyed every weary mile of it and arrived at camp with 3 more silky marten to add to our already fine collection . . . .*"

"*The next day, we regretfully locked the little cabin door and pushed skis across the basin towards the valley, far below. At the edge of the last basin, we stopped and looked back. The two dogs turned, too, and I am sure they shared our regrets.*"

By the fall of 1944, Bill had built up a full year's worth of annual leave and decided to run an extensive prospect line for marten. He teamed up with a fellow FS employee, Fred Rixey, who had never trapped marten before, but Bill liked his attitude and knew he was a hard worker. While waiting for marten season to open, they ran traplines for coyotes, gray fox, and bobcats each day after work and on weekends. Bill said the subspecies of 'cats in that area of the Sierras were called "pallid" and he said they were of the finest quality of any he had ever trapped. Marten season finally opened, and he and Fred drove as far as they could in a car to the snow line. From there, they skied to their cabin at 7,000' and arrived around 6:30 that evening.

Bill with a 7-day catch of coyote, pallid bobcat, and marten from a prospect line on skis.

(Photo courtesy of Marlene Rider)

Bill prepared supper that first night and he said, *"Fred looked wide-eyed at the amount of food I prepared and stacked on the table, but it all melted away before two trail-sharpened appetites."* The next morning, they left early and Bill began to instruct Fred in the art of marten trapping and set locations. They covered a lot of country on skis and only made sets at key locations since Bill wanted to cover as much country as possible in preparation for a future big-time trapline. They noted marten and weasel were the main furbearers found at that altitude, along with a few mountain coyotes and pallid 'cats. Pine squirrels, or chickarees, as Bill called them, flying squirrels, mice, and shrews were the main foods for the predators. After a few days, the marten catch began to pile up and one day while they checked their traps, they were surprised to find a freak or "sport" marten, which was a mutation, in one of their sets. Bill described the marten. "... *I carefully examined the animal and noted the unusual fur depth, and was impressed with the general golden shade of the fur instead of the usual rich mummy and snuff browns. So unusual was the complete color scheme, that I made some careful notes. Face mask was a stone gray with sprinkling of cocoa guard hairs; beige at forehead, blending to cream-white at ears; sides of neck showing sprinkle of silver-cream guard hairs; back of head a warm brown with underfur of blue-fox blue. Dorsal strip along back a rich mummy brown, lower sides a rich golden-tan with sepia wash, here and there; flanks golden tan, the underfur of back sides and flanks blending from a mouse blue to cream white. The throat and all of ventral strip a pale golden-orange, with burnt orange at belly glands. Legs shading from snuff brown to otter brown; feet ivory cream. Tail a pale cocoa brown, darkening near tip, underfur of tail a pale beige; the very tail tip terminating in a bunch of long silvery hairs. Truly a beautiful animal and I felt like I was looking at some exotic sable from an unknown land.*" He told Fred this was a "1 in 10,000 catch."

They continued their prospect line until 2 weeks were gone and decided to wait until after the first of the year to use up the remaining week of their leave.

They resumed trapping on January 15, 1945. By then, the snow was very deep and Bill noted it sometimes took hours to get to the top of some ridges with the skis, but only a few seconds to ski down the other side.

Bill began to have enough confidence in Fred's abilities as a trapper and skier to let him run separate lines so they could cover more country and catch more martens. One night, Fred returned from his line and was disappointed he had "toed" a marten which had escaped from the trap at one of his sets. Bill consoled him and told him that it would more than likely be recaught as marten are not known to be as wary as some furbearers, even after being caught, before.

On the 24th, Fred returned to camp, all smiles, with a match to the first "sport" marten, caught in the same basin. The color scheme was similar, but the depth of the fur and the color schemes were not quite as desirable as the first one. It was not the same age as the first, either, and Bill wondered if there was a true mutation strain occurring in that area.

Their time used up, Bill and Fred pulled all their traps and regretfully returned to the valley below to their "real jobs". Bill nicknamed the basin where the 2 sport marten were taken, Mystery Basin. They sold the 2 mutation martens for $60 each, far more than the other martens they trapped, sold for.

Normal-colored marten, center, flanked on each side by the mutation martens trapped in Mystery Basin. Note the white paws and larger orange throat patches of the mutations. (Bill Nelson photo)

Coyote, marten, pallid bobcat, 'coon, weasel, and gray fox trapped by
Bill and Fred Rixey on a 3-week prospect line with skis in the Sierras.
(Photo courtesy of Marlene Rider)

SKIING FOR SIERRA SABLES

Three years of part-time prospect trapping for marten on skis in the Sierras led up to a full-time, all-season trapline which started on October 20, 1945. Bill had made arrangements with a local resort owner to use his lodge as a base camp. The lodge was located about 7 miles from town and at an elevation of 5,700'. From there, he had 5 other spike cabins spread out over his long 73-mile trapline. It took him 6-8 days, depending on the weather, to complete the loop and then he would return to the base camp for a brief rest and to put up his catch of martens.

Edith at the base-camp lodge with Judy on her lap and Mutt looking away.
(Photo courtesy of Ruth Peterson)

For traveling the deep snow of the Sierras, Bill revived the use of long skis or "Sierra Snow-shoes" or "Sierra Shoes," for short. They had been introduced into that region by Scandinavian gold miners during the mid-1850s. Later, they were adopted by marten trappers and even mailmen, as this was the only mode of transportation during the winter. Bill had to seek out a few of the old-timers in that area who still remembered how to make them. The Sierra Shoes were made from the light, but strong and flexible heartwood of Douglas fir trees. They had thin, but supple tips and carefully- whittled tapered grooves, extending from toe to heel. They ranged in lengths from 8-11' and were much wider and thicker than conventional sporting skis, which were worthless in deep fluffy snow. Ski bindings were not used on these modified skis. Rather, an open leather harness that allowed one's feet to break free, quickly, during a fall. Various ski waxes or "dopes" were used, depending on temperature and snow conditions. A single 6'-long "Screw Pole" with a "button" of live oak on the bottom was used instead of a pair of regular ski poles to gain momentum when skiing downhill, for balance when making turns and manuevers, and as a brake, when descending.

Bill's mode of transportation for trapping marten in the Sierras consisted of cruising skis, "Sierra Snowshoes," trail webs, and bear-paw webs.
(Photo courtesy of Marlene Rider)

Bill mentioned the use of Sierra Shoes had not really been used much since 1911. He lamented that fact and gave 3 reasons for it: the current generation lacked the ambition and fortitude to do it; a lost art like that was hard to revive unless it had many champions; and there was little or no need for that type of transportation in the Sierras, anymore. He stated his revival of the Sierra Shoes for trapping marten created a few local newspaper articles and some radio coverage. A couple years later, he wrote an article about these unique skis.

Like common downhill skis, snowshoes or "webs," could not be used in those deep snows, either. Bill learned this the hard way when he once traveled 11 miles carrying a 65-pound pack on his back while wearing 60" Yukon webs. He sunk up to his knees with every step. It took him 8 hours to travel the 11 miles and he arrived at camp long after dark only to find the cabin almost covered with snow, and he spent another hour shoveling down to the door, just to get in. He said the locals of the Sierras called snowshoes or webs "trampers." He stated, *"You sure do tramp on a pair of webs. In fact, you tramp the heart right out of yourself. Go ahead and use them if you wish, but do not think for one minute that a good man on skis cannot operate over twice as much trapline in mountainous regions."* He did occasionally use webs, but only on crusted snow or a well-packed snow base. He also carried a pair of short bear-paw webs on his pack, just in case of an emergency.

Bill's skiing outfit consisted of a pair of 7' cruising skis, 2 pairs of 8' skis, one extremely light pair of 10-1/2' Sierra Shoes, and 2 pairs of full-width 10-1/2' Sierra Shoes.

A standard item in Bill's pack was a soot-blackened can with a wire bail and an extension wire for hanging the can from his screw pole over a fire to boil tea, at mid-day. This, along with a lunch, several chocolate bars for added energy, and his pipe and tobacco rejuvenated him while enjoying the vast mountain scenery.

Edith stayed at the base camp lodge while Bill ran his lines. About every week to 10 days, she would ski into town to pick up their mail, fresh meat and other groceries, and to catch up on news from the outside world. It was a 14-mile round trip and Bill commented she was in shape and could handle the trip with a 35- pound pack on her back, with ease. She even ran a few marten sets, herself.

I will not describe the marten sets and locations Bill used, as they will be described in the next chapter on marten trapping. Rather, I will highlight some of the quotes he used to describe some of his experiences along that full-time marten line and some of the scenes he saw. Regarding his daily workplace, he said, "*There is nothing on earth as magnificent as the sight of a great snowy mountain range stretching endlessly as far as the eyes can see. The grandeur of such a range in its winter sleep fills you with something you cannot write or speak. You can only feel it and think about it . . . Tough trails when the snow often piles up to over 15' on the level, where drifts on the lee sides of divides mount to from 40-80'. Trails along which the lone trapper dare not make a single mistake, as it might very well be his last . . . No few old-time marten trappers have come to the end of their journey along the great white ranges of the Sierras, the Rockies, and the Cascades.*"

Bill and Edith had 2 dogs at that time: Mutt, a smaller mixed-breed variety, and Judy, a larger Australian shepherd. Bill usually took one, and sometimes both of them, on his lines for company and in case of a mishap. He trusted they would run back to the base camp and bark a distress call for Edith. Usually though, he left Judy with Edith, for company.

Bill described spending all morning slowly ascending a pass on skis and how it felt to reach the top. "... *It was afternoon when I neared the 8,000' pass and wearily picked a spot for lunch. Squatting there in the snow and smoking my pipe, I felt refreshed as I looked out over the seemingly endless rolls of the Sierra Nevadas. Great snow-draped domes, spires, and ridges stretched north and south as far as the eye could see. To the east, lay the great high Nevada deserts and to the west, the rim of the Coast Range dimly showed. Shifting my position, I could see Mt. Lassen in the distant north and beyond that, Mt. Shasta, the "White Lady" of the Sierras. Nearer in, countless other prominent peaks, many that were familiar to me ...*."

Continuing along the main divide ridge and sometimes descending into an alpine basin or lake, he would continue. "*Nearer the end of a day, after a bad storm had passed and the sky cleared, the sun to the west would appear to be a great blood-red disk surrounded by streaks of gold, purple, and red. As darkness gathered, the canyons below would be shrouded in a deep purple haze and here and there, a peak would stand out starkly white in the gathering gloom as the now-hidden sun would send a slating bit of light against it.*

A few times while traveling the main ridges, a dense low layer of clouds would come in against the summits and send strange wisps of vapor over the saddled passes that cut the main divides. At times, I would be above this mass with a clear sky above me and then coming to a pass, I would actually be wading in the clouds. Walking through those sniffling vapors made me feel like I was watching the smokes from geologic fires in a world just being born."

After being out for 6 or more days on the marten lines and spending the nights in line camps with Mutt, Bill described what it was like to finally arrive at the base camp with a pack full of marten pelts and the anticipation of seeing Edith, eating a home-cooked meal, a long hot bath, and lounging in front of the fireplace. "... *Nearing main camp late that evening, we both quickened our pace. Soon, I could smell pine smoke, then I could see the sprawling form of the lodge. Blue smoke cured a bit, then traced a line up through the snow from the tall chimney. The wife's big camp dog, Judy, barked a happy challenge that echoed through* the still valley, and then she came bounding and plunging through the deep snow to meet us. Edith waved from the open door, a happy setting for a weary trapper and his cocky little line dog that had struggled along in my ski trails for 6 long days. Seventy-three miles of the roughest cross-country the Sierras had to offer, lay behind us. Sable furs were snuggled in my pack."

After spending almost 60 days on the long marten lines, Bill took a few days off and he and Edith celebrated a very memorable Christmas at the lodge. ". . . The day before Christmas, I made the 14-mile round trip to town and brought back an over-sized turkey, other fresh meats, nuts, candy, a brown bottle of Yuletide cheer, and all the trimmings. This was to be a real Alpine Holiday. We already had presents purchased in late September placed around a beautiful red-fir tree in the den room . . . There a bit below the summits of the Sierra Nevadas, we enjoyed the finest Christmas we have ever known. Presents, tinsel, and paper were scattered around the tree and the kitchen table sagged under the weight of food that would have fed a round dozen hungry men. Even the 2 dogs groaned and yawned before the crackling fire, numb with the lazy feeling that comes from too much turkey and dressing. Along the rafters in one wing of the lodge, a long line of silky sables hung from hooks. A few bundles of white weasels flanked them along with some pallid bobcats and large mountain coyotes I had taken before marten trapping became a full-time job. The weather was fair that Christmas night and a great silver moon rested along the purple rim of the summit. Above the cabin, the sparkle of the snow on the trees, and stars that seemed so close you felt like trying to touch them. It was a good Christmas . . . ."

Although Bill wrote about the good times and breathtaking scenery he and Edith had experienced on that memorable trapline, it was not all fun and easy going. He vividly described the onset of those Sierra storms that could dump up to 4' of snow in one night and cover his pole sets that were chest-high above the snow before the storms hit. "Many times I have seen the first front of a Sierra Storm coming in over south and west ridges, the low black squall clouds rolling like angry breakers along a storm-swept seashore. A dark mass of ugly, ragged clouds pushed by a screaming wind that hits the divides and rolls back in rushing eddies and updrafts that snaps and uproots trees.

Wave after wave, they attack. First, a low thunder of sounds, then a rushing roar that fades away, only to return. I have seen the ragged fingers of clouds sweeping the high basins at tree-top level. As the storm gains force, the wind is a screeching fury that would whip you off your feet, were you at a high saddle or along an open ridge. Even along the basins, you will have to lean sharply to stay on your skis while trees will be going down, crashing to the snow with deceiving speed. At times like this, it is a welcome sight to see the form of a cabin loom up through the storm.

Bill all loaded up and ready to head out on his 6-day, 73-mile marten trapline. Note the bear-paw webs lashed to his pack basket for emergency.
(Bill Nelson photo)

This wind will last from 1-6 hours before the storm center moves in and the sudden lull after the banshee wail of that howling-wind demon seems to pound at your eardrums. Then the snow moves in with its strange whispering sounds; a great smothering blanket of downy white that blots out everything but your ski tips. Now, there are no longer any landmarks to stand out in-friendly and familiar relief. You are very much alone in a strange white world that is pitched high in a great storm center, and I assure you that you had better know your way around. I know, because I have been there, many times . . . Traveling in these blinding storms gives one a strange sensation. You see nothing but white on all sides. You see but a-short distance ahead; sometimes, not even past the ski tips. If you are riding the skis on a fairly fast run, tree trunks glide by you like dark, speeding ghosts that are bent on reaching the summits above before you reach the basins, below. Your skis make a strange whispering sound in the snow and send up 2 sets of powdery plumes . . . ." Bill told Don Paul of once incident where he was crossing a pass and the wind was blowing so hard he had to crouch and crawl across it on his hands and knees with the dog, under him.

Bill suffered a mishap along his lines, one day. ". . . On a sizzling run into the lower basins, I took the first bad spill of the season. I was very weary and my timing was poor. Half way down, I swooped into a high roll and went spinning through the air. The heavy pack made my bouncing 100-foot fall none too comfortable and I ended up in a smother of snow. The worst part of the spill was a broken ski, and this time of all times I had, much against my better judgement, left the little bear-paw webs at main camp. I had tried to cut down my load due to the deep and fluffy snow. Well, it was a good lesson for me and I had a heart-breaking 2 miles into camp two with the broken bit of ski that drove into the snow at every step . . . Next day, a slow and torturous 9-mile trip to main camp for now skis and the bear-paws." That fall, and several others, took a toll on Bill throughout the following years. Don Paul said Bill's back pain would flare up from time to time when he trapped with Bill, a few years later. Bill would lay on his stomach and insist that Don remove his shoes and then walk on his back. By walking on certain areas of his back, relief would finally come and Bill would be fine until the next episode. This seemed like a rather harsh chiropractic treatment, but it worked and Bill would not go to a doctor.

Bill related another scary incident to Don that had happened during an early fall prospecting trip. He was carrying a smaller pack and following a narrow game trail up into the rim rocks. The trail became so narrow that he could no longer continue forward nor could he turn back around. Looking down, it was hundreds of feet to the canyon floor. He had to fight off panic and dizziness if he continued to look down. Looking up, it appeared the top of the cliff might be 20' above him. The cliff wall was fairly straight and smooth and he noticed several small trees and bushes growing out of the wall. With a mighty effort and thrust, he grabbed for each tree and bush and clawed and kicked his way to the top which luckily for him turned out to be a flat plateau with a way down on the other side. After realizing what he had just done and what the consequences could have been, he became weak and nauseated and he vomited. He had cheated death- this time.

Edith once accompanied him on one of his lines from the base camp to the first line camp. She had remarked how she would like to be out in a real Sierra storm, just to say she'd done it. That day, a bad storm did come in and by afternoon, she told Bill they could reach camp at any time, as far as she was concerned. A short time later, they did, much to the relief of them both.

Bill caught, but lost, another sport or mutation marten that season in Mystery Basin, but he recaught it a month later, about a mile away. This confirmed what he had told Fred Rixey the year before about "toeing" marten and recatching them, later. This sport marten was even larger and better-colored than the other two.

Bill continued to trap until Easter 1946 when the snow became too crusty and dangerous to travel anymore and snow slides began to occur. This was the longest continuous trapline he had, or would ever run - almost 6 months. He stated he had trapped more martens that season by himself than were officially reported for the whole state of CA, but he did not reveal the exact number. He also stated he had received an average of $30 more per pelt than what the state average was, too. By matching similar pelts, he received $50-80, each, for them and he sorted out the lower-grade culls and shipped them to a fur company in St. Louis where he received from $27-40 each. He sold the 3rd mutation marten for $80 and later regretted selling the 3 mutations for $200 when he could have later received $200 each. He told Jack Harris about a shrewd marketing strategy he had come up with. He would get all dressed up and head for a larger-town restaurant (probably in Reno, Oroville, or Sacramento). He would put a matched pair of marten pelts under his long coat and walk in and strike up a conversation with a classy-looking, well-dressed lady. When he thought the time was right, he would show her the fine marten furs which sometimes resulted in a sale of $100 for the pair. If not, he still had the pleasure of good company.

Remembering Edith's dream of a sable choker scarf, Bill saved back 4 of his best pelts and had them made into two 2-piece scarves. ". . . But, she decided that 2 sable chokers were too much for a trapper's wife, so we sold one of them. But believe me, I would hate to be caught so much as ruffling a hair on the one she still has locked away."

Bill summed up his 4th season of marten trapping, which would be his last, although he didn't know it at the time. *"To me, the marten trapline is the most interesting that I can follow. It is the most rugged and dangerous trapping one can tackle. When I say this, I am speaking of long-line professional marten trapping. I mean, it is tough. Show me a professional marten trapper and I will show you one tough hombre . . . I had to travel over country that even the hardened natives of the Sierra Nevadas would not even consider traveling during the storm periods of the winter months,*

Bill with just a few of the martens he trapped during the 6-month season in the Sierras, 1945-46. (Bill Nelson photo)

and until they became better acquainted with me, they were placing bets on just how long I would last, up there." After returning to Downieville that spring, an old resident looked him up and down, carefully, and said, "By golly, Bill, you are a tough guy. You had to be." Bill stated this was one of the best compliments he had ever received. He had skied almost 2,000 miles during that 6-month venture.

Bill and Edith intended to come back there for another season, or maybe more. Years later he wrote, *". . . Some day in the near future, I am going back. My five pairs of skis are stored in a little mountain town, waiting for me. This time, though, I am taking a full-time partner with me. I have been a "lone wolf" along the far-back traplines too many times."* He also added, *". . . She often asks me when I am going into the high country again for the marten hunt. I think she wants that other scarf back, or perhaps an even better one with 3 skins instead of 2. . . ."*

They returned to IA later that spring, never to return, but the memories of those years spent in CA, and especially in the Sierras, left a lasting impression on both of them and almost every conversation I had with them would lead to a story about their experiences in the Sierras.

EPILOGUE

Bill would be pleased to know the Sierra Snowshoes were later remembered and their use has been revived. An article by Robert Laxalt entitled, "Golden Ghosts Of The Lost Sierra", appeared in the September 1973 issue of NATIONAL GEOGRAPHIC magazine on pages 332-353, a few months after Bill died. The article presented a history of the area around Downieville and surrounding mining towns and described and illustrated the Sierra Snowshoes that were so important in traveling that country during the winter and provided recreation for the residents in the form of downhill skiing races.

William Berry was an avid skier, ski historian, and a member of the U.S. Ski Hall of Fame who helped establish the William B. Berry Western American Ski Sport Museum at Boreal Ridge, near Donners Pass along Interstate 80, west of Reno, NV. Specimens of Sierra Snowshoes, old photographs of the era, etc. are displayed at the museum, as well as other historic skiing memorabilia. Mr. Berry was the one who dubbed the area around Downieville, the "Lost Sierra" and after spending considerable time and effort researching historical books and documents and interviewing old-timers in the region, he wrote a book, LOST SIERRA- GOLD, GHOSTS, AND SKIS, 1991, 227 pages, which is a complete written and photographic history of the area, including the origin, use, and decline of the Sierra Snowshoes. Unfortunately, Bill Nelson was not mentioned in the book, nor any information about marten trapping or marten trappers using the Shoes. The book is available from: Emigrant Trail Museum, 12593 Donner Pass Rd, Truckee, CA 96161, phone: 530-582-7892.

Most recently, a demonstration of "longboarding," as it is now called, was presented during the 2002 Winter Olympics in Salt Lake City, UT. It was well received by the audience from all over the world and was covered by both TV and newspaper media. It was noted that "longboard" races now occur every winter in the "Lost Sierra" country between local teams and teams from the Tahoe/Reno and other areas.

And so, Bill's efforts to promote and publicize the use of the Sierra Snowshoes were finally successful, even though it took many years to occur and he did not live to see it.

Downtown Downieville, CA, Labor Day weekend, 2002.
(Sherm Blom photo)

Sierra Buttes, or "Buttes" as Bill called them in some of his articles. A prominent landmark in the area. (Sherm Blom photo)

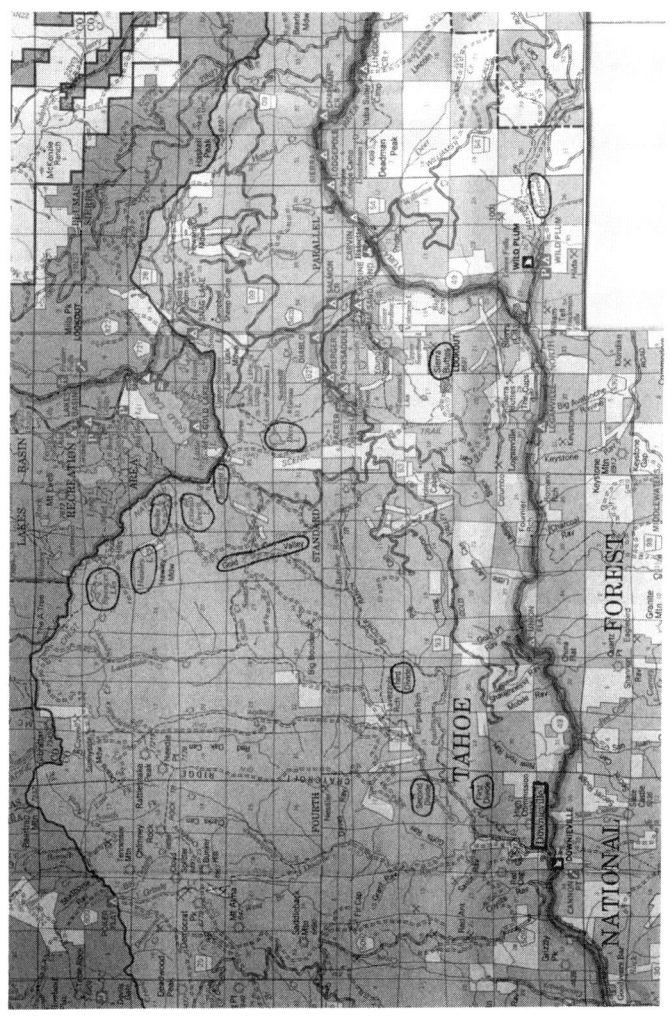

Map of Downieville, CA area where Bill trapped marten.
Locations circled are places he mentioned in his articles.
Today, roads and trails crisscross the area,
including the Pacific Crest Trail

Chapter 6

MARTEN LORE AND TRAPPING

During one of our visits, Bill told me he had begun to write a manuscript for a book on trapping marten and other alpine furbearers. He obviously did not finish it before he died, and I asked Fuller Laugeman if he had received the manuscript when he purchased Bill's lure business, and he said he hadn't. Therefore, I will present a brief outline of some marten lore, set locations, and actual sets that Bill used, based on information from several of his articles on marten.

Bill had some advice for those who even thought about marten trapping, let alone actually doing it. *"I do not recommend marten trapping to any man other than he that is really fixed with a true ambition to buck those mountain trails, the storms, and the backaches. Full-fledged marten trapping is often heart-breaking work; dangerous and lonely work. On the other hand, it is the most interesting and thrilling type of trapping one can possibly do. Many and many an old-time marten trapper took his last trails and his last long sleep under the snows of the alpine country. But, they must have loved it. I can well see why they did. The high country presents the most beautiful scenery on earth. This, and the thrill of the marten hunt can made a man do foolish things . . . Long-line marten work is not recommended to any but the experienced man. To go into the storm-swept alpine regions for days on end without any outside contact is life less than foolhardy, unless you know what you are doing and how to do it. The beginner will do well to work into marten trapping by degrees. There are sections that allow a bit of marten work without the extremely long-line work. One or two-day trips can be made and the needed experience gained. Remember, it is not all riding skis and tending traps. You have to know the very real dangers that are there, and how to avoid them. You have to spend a great deal of time preparing for the marten lines . . . ."*

Bill described marten life zones and habitat in the Sierra Nevadas as starting at the 6,000' level and containing such trees as red fir, western white pine, mountain hemlock, lodgepole, and quaking aspen. In some areas, limber pine and fox-tail pine would also be present.

He listed chickarees and alpine flying squirrels as the main winter foods of martens. During the summer, they fed mostly on mice and voles, chipmunks, golden-mantled ground squirrels, and "digger squirrels." Alpine basins, canyon heads, and lake basins were good habitat for these prey animals and during the winter, lodgepoles and red firs held the most chickarees and flying squirrels.

Bill noted that marten often migrate and leave the trapper with barren traplines unless there is an abundance of rodents available for their food. "... *The habit of marten migration must be considered. A wise trapper will have 2 well-separated marten areas prospected and ready for business. This might save the season in the event of a mass migration in one area or the other. Generally, however, any marten migration can be directly linked to food supply . . . .*" He also stressed that martens were unusually active before and after storms, similar to other furbearers and predators. Using this knowledge, he sometimes retraced his lines after a big storm to capitalize on this "before and after" movement.

He pointed out that marten are not cunning or trap-shy and could be trapped in uncovered traps, provided there was something at the set they wanted. Sets that included plenty of nose and eye appeal. Contrary to some theories of marten trapping, he advocated the use of lures in addition to baits. He stated that many martens would by-pass sets where bait, alone, was used. Several times, he had seen tracks in the snow where martens had turned at right angles from where they were traveling and head 200-300' directly towards one of his well-scented sets. During the long 6-month season he ran in the Sierra during 1945-46, he used 1 quart of call lures and another pint of gland lure to make his big catch. He said he probably wouldn't have taken one-third the marten he did, without lures.

No matter what species of animal he was trapping, Bill always stressed the importance of set locations. "... *This principle of set location dictates how the marten lines must be placed. Actually, it is simply selecting the primary ridges, or summits, that best tie in to the better basin areas."* As for specific set locations, he described many: denning areas of thick growth of timber in basins, canyon heads, and small cup basins; along rocky cliffs and divides; saddles, rims, and slide areas; main connecting divides and rims above alpine lakes; meadows bordering thick growths of timber, drainages entering lakes and meadows; timbered fingers extending into lakes and meadows; small streams connecting timber and thickets with meadows and lakes; shallow saddles or dips on ridges and especially those with fingers of timber leading up to them; piles of downed timber in slides; halfway up deep canyons and draws of timber that lead to ridge tops; at the heads of canyons; fingers of timber coming up on both sides of a ridge; main ridge saddles; intersections of smaller ridges with main ones; points of timber jutting out into a main ridge; heads of slides; drainages running off basins; and rim-rock thickets. In his own words, he described a near-perfect set location. *". . . Coming to a knife-edged ridge, I turned and followed a point of small fir trees to a saddle cut deep by canyons coming in from each side. There in a clump of mountain hemlock, I made a set that I knew was a killer for any marten in that section. Travelers were sure to hit it and any hunting marten working the canyons were also sure to visit such a place . . . ."* And another. *". . . On a bench of land, I made a spike set on a lone hemlock that stood near the rim of the slope . . . ."*

    Bill used mostly pole sets for trapping marten and called them, *"king."* He did use cubby and spike sets at times, but only if the set location did not lend itself to using a pole set. He said pole sets offered the best in eye and nose appeal and once trapped, a marten would be held away from the tree to avoid getting pitch on its fur and kept away from mice and shrews that could damage the pelt by gnawing on it. He stressed setting any marten set at least 4' above the current snow level as some snowstorms would dump that much snow in one falling and cover the set, rendering it useless. When selecting a tree for making a pole set, he preferred a live tree with good dense top cover to shelter the set, but not too low a shelter as to prevent the set from being seen from a long distance. For the pole, he cut one 5' long and 3" at the base. He nailed the pole to the tree, chest-high, with 2 nails, butt end 24" past the trunk and touching the ground, and the slender end extending 3' past the trunk at the upper end, 4' above snowline. If the tree trunk was extremely wide, a longer pole would have to be cut. Fourteen inches past the trunk on the high side of the pole, he flattened a section of the pole with his hatchet and placed the trap on it. He preferred a waxed #2 Victor jump trap, set hair-trigger. He secured the trap to the flattened section of the pole with a single twist of black stovepipe wire. The trap chain was shortened and wired out towards the end of the pole from the trap. This was to keep the trapped marten from swinging back and reaching the trunk for footing. At the very end of the pole, he wired a chickaree or flying squirrel by the head, hanging it down 6" below the pole. He warned the end of the pole with the bait should not be close to another tree, brush, or limbs, so a marten could approach the bait from that end without passing over the trap. He also stressed keeping that end of the pole at least 4' above the snow level to keep martens from grabbing the bait from the bottom. Hung in this manner, the slightest breeze would cause the bait to move and provide maximum eye appeal. The set was lured by soaking call lure into the tail of the bait animal and also well above the pole on the trunk of the tree. At the base of the tree, he smeared some gland lure, bits of fur, meat and blood from the slit belly of the bait animal before he hung it from the pole. As final eye appeal, he took a claw tool and scratched off bits of tree bark around the base of the tree and under the pole.

Bill removing one of the mutation marten from a pole set in Mystery Basin. Note the white back paws. (Bill Nelson photo)

Even when he used cubby sets, he liked to prop a pole from the snowline up to the cubby and the trap was set on a flattened section of the pole, just in front of the cubby entrance. Bait was placed inside at the back of the cubby and lure was smeared on the bait. Gland lure and eye appeal were applied as with a pole set.

He liked to use spike sets at lone-tree set locations. Two large spikes were nailed, chest-high, into a tree about 3-4" apart and level. The trap was wired to these spikes with a single twist of stovepipe wire and the trap chain had to be fastened directly to the tree trunk. Another spike was nailed 2' above the trap and the bait was wired to it. He covered the bait loosely with green boughs to reduce detection by birds. Call lure was smeared on the bait and gland lure and eye appeal were applied as with the other 2 sets. The biggest disadvantage with the spike set was fur damage from tree pitch and a good majority of martens trapped at spike sets were still alive when the sets were checked, he said.

One must keep in mind the marten methods that Bill used were in mountainous areas of the West. Some of what he advocated would not, of course, apply to flatter "northwoods" areas of the Great Lakes states nor eastern and New England areas. But, the sets, luring and baiting strategies, and general set locations would still apply.

Bill summed up marten trapping as follows. "... Other than the Russian sable, itself, I know of no animal that wears a fur as beautiful as that of the marten ... The sight of one of these American sables swinging free and clean from a set makes up for hardships you have gone through that day, and it makes

Bill removing a marten
from a spike set.
(Bill Nelson photo)

you forget the tough trails of yesterday. When the end of the season is at hand and you proudly examine and gloat over a fine string of these glossy- brown furs, you know that you are looking at a catch of royal furbearers that very few trappers have had the pleasure of even seeing. Though marten trapping is, without exception, the toughest and most dangerous that you can tackle, it is a most fascinating game. It has rich rewards that cannot alone be measured with dollars and cents."

Chapter 7

BACK TO IOWA

After spending some of the best years of their lives in CA, Bill and Edith returned to IA the spring of 1946. An event to come would change Bill's life, forever, second only to his marriage to Edith. He had made arrangements to have all his traps and equipment shipped back to IA by rail since a line ran right through Farmington and national trucklines were nonexistent, then. The train caught fire and all of Bill's freight was burned. He described the tragedy as follows. "... *Over 600 traps, over half being Newhouse, went up in smoke at a railroad siding at Bakersfield, CA during the early fall of 1946. A lifetime collection of handsome and beautifully-finished one-piece fur forms also went up in smoke when that car burned, plus many other bits of trapline equipment.*" Words cannot describe how he must have felt about this tragic and very expensive loss. Not to be conquered, he teamed up with one of his long-time buddies, Forrest Rider, on a full-time trapline in the Farmington area. They had to use Forrest's traps and equipment which were not near enough for Bill's mode of trapping, but in spite of that, they started fox trapping the first week of November. After a few days, Forrest trapped an animal he couldn't identify. Bill told him it was a badger, which was very rare in that part of IA. Later in the season, Bill trapped another one, about a mile from there. It rained a lot that first week, but they still trapped up to 10 foxes a day, but lost up to 6 more a day to thieves which really irritated them.

They used a Model-A car to tend their traplines and Bill remarked it got a real work-out. "*We sure puddled through some rugged spots along abandoned old country roads and lanes. The Model-A wheezed and staggered through some of the gosh-awfullest places you ever saw. We went where no other car tracks showed and crossed wash-outs with fractions-of-an-inch to spare. With fenders flapping wildly and the hood cover spread like the wings of a swooping hawk, we would rush a low muddy swale. We would bounce, splash, clatter, and bang with reckless abandon through* spots that would have sunk a jeep. That old car groaned in every joint and when we stopped, I'll sure swear I could hear it give a deep sigh of relief. But, it took us where we wanted to go, regardless of where it might be or how much it might have rained."

The regular fur season opened on November 10th, and they began to set traps for mink, 'coon, muskrat, etc. along the waterways so their traplines consisted of about 60% land and 40% water. "Most of our mink lines were placed in semi-prairie country that was crisscrossed with a network of unmarked roads. I am sure that we became confused at least 20 times in that tangle of roads. It was painful at times, but it also held a lot of comedy. In fact, when we actually made the rounds without becoming mixed up, it called for a small celebration. This celebration was usually in the form of congratulations passed back and forth and a solemn nip from the 'frostbite-lotion' which we carried back of the seat with the assorted scent and bait containers."

Late in December, they sold their mink for a $20 average and muskrats for a $2 average. At the end of January 1947, they sold another batch of 200 mixed furs, excluding the foxes. Forrest had to quit trapping to begin preparing for the spring season with his nursery business, but Bill continued to trap fox in new locations and to conduct some experiments with new sets and lures. Most of the new sets were made in frozen ground, so he had to cut through the frozen layer of sod with an ax to reach unfrozen loose soil to set in and utilize his dirt antifreeze system. "This was slow work, but once a set was completed, it rolled over the red fox as nicely as any early November set."

Edith even accompanied him, sometimes. "... *My wife made several trips with me and I began to give her instructions in fox trapping. That she will ever make use of the knowledge she*

Edith sometimes went with Bill on his fox lines. Here she is with 3 foxes taken in a group setting. (Photo courtesy of Marlene Rider)

gained is open to doubt. She much prefers the marten traplines, or so she claims. I guess the winter charm of the alpine countries has won her for good."

By the end of January, Bill pulled all his traps and he took an inventory of the foxes that were left. He noted foxes were changing their travel routes and wandered far from their regular crossings during the approaching breeding season. He advised trappers not to learn fox crossings and set locations during this period, but rather during September and early October. After surveying the country, Bill was satisfied he had left sufficient breeding stock, and so ended a successful season. Although he didn't reveal the total take of foxes, he was disappointed at the price they received for them. *"Needless to say, it was quite a tumble from $100 marten to fox that were bringing a bit under the $3 mark."* After trapping 6 seasons in remote areas of CA with little or no competition, he was quite disgusted with what trapping had become in IA. *"... I am most certainly damn-well tired of stumbling over fences and discarded tin cans and wire, tired of the over-trapped and poorly-managed trapping that the state of IA now offers, tired of bridges that are visited by 4 to 8 sets of trappers, tired of posted personal property, stray dogs, stray cats, and stray trap thieves...."*

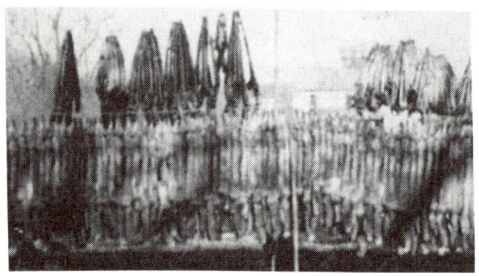

Part of the catch of furs trapped by Bill and Forrest Rider during the 1946-47 season on a 60% land, 40% water trapline. (Bill Nelson photo)

After that 1946-47 trapping season, Bill began to form the business he would become famous for in the years to come. He began to advertise his lure formulas, his dirt-antifreeze method, and personal trapping instructions in several trapping magazines. A short time after that, he began to manufacture and sell his famous line of animal and fish lures. All of these will be discussed, in depth, in subsequent chapters of this book. He also began to write more articles about his past experiences in wildcrafting, fishing, and trapping, as well as more instructional-type articles on these subjects. He continued his wildcrafting activities throughout the spring, summer, and early fall months.

It was during this period, too, that he came up with a scheme to continue trapping by using other trappers' traps and operating with them on a student-partner basis. They would furnish the traps and equipment, vehicle and gas and he would provide the lures, bait, country to trap, meals, place to put up furs, and of course, on-the-line trapping instructions which were far more informative and educational than his one-day instructions. All other expenses were split, as well as the profits from furs after expenses, of course. He wrote, ". . . *I have never completely outfitted since then, though I am again making a start in that direction. Since that outfit went up in smoke, I have more or less operated with trappers on a student-partner basis. Some of this has been good, some fair, and some of it, very bad."*

Don Paul was a student-partner of Bill's during the seasons of 1948-49 and 1949-50. I was very fortunate to interview him and his recall of those 2 seasons was astounding, after over 50 years. Don was no stranger to fox trapping. The year before, he had trapped fox with Harry Ferguson of Willoughby, OH, the OH State Champion Trapper, and Don learned a lot from him. Harry had used a mower sickle-type earth anchor for anchoring fox traps instead of a trap stake, and what was probably the forerunner to all the various earth anchors being used, today.

The first season, Bill and Don trapped red fox around Farmington, using Don's Ford car. Bill insisted on driving, though, since he knew the road systems and drove very fast to make the best use of driving time. Don said Bill would often drive 60-65 mph and since there were no speed limits in those days, he would sometimes reach 80-85 mph on good roads, but he was an excellent judge of speed, distance, and timing and knew when to slow down and when to accelerate, again. Bill also knew how far he could go on field roads, crossing streams and gullies, and during rainy weather. If he did get stuck, he would stop, and they would put sticks and brush under the tires and make it out before they really got stuck.

They ran 3-day lines and each line was laid out in circles or loops. A day's line consisted of 3-4 stops, and they would get out of the car and walk each loop of that stop. Each of them would check every other set so there was no doubling-up or duplication of efforts. Don was 27 years old that first season, and Bill was 40. Don said he could not keep up with Bill. He stated, "He covered ground faster than anyone I have ever known on his steady 'high-ball' pace. In spite of his endurance, swift gait, and ability to cover much ground in little time, I never remember seeing him run. It seemed to be unnecessary. He could be making excellent time and seemingly remain unhurried and breathing easily. No strain . . . He moved silently . . . You could be with him on a trapline, then separate, and sometime later, he would appear, seemingly out of nowhere. He could remain almost invisible, when he chose to. He sure knew how to take advantage of the surrounding terrrain to remain unnoticed until he was almost upon you."

Don had mostly Victor #2 coilspring traps, and a lot of them were already equipped with the sickle-type earth anchors. The rest of the traps were fastened to wooden stakes which Bill showed Don how to make from dogwood or other tough hardwood limbs. He selected a limb with a knot on top for strength when pounding it into the ground. For added strength, he wrapped 2 wraps of annealed wire around the stake, about 2" below the top and twisted them tight with a plier. This helped prevent the stake from splitting while driving it. A rough point was cut on the bottom of the stake with an ax, and they were good to go.

They each carried a canvas pack with their traps, tools, lures and bait, dry dirt, etc. Each morning before they left the house, it was Don's job to liberally spray the packs, inside and out, as well as their gloves and trapping tools, with fox urine. "We truly smelled like a fox", Don said. For footwear, Bill wore Gokey waterproof leather boots and Don wore leather rubber-bottomed ones. When it rained heavily, they both wore ankle-tight hip boots and rolled them down below the knees for easier walking. Although they were trapping fox, Bill could not resist setting a few mink traps when they crossed creeks and streams.

Besides red fox, they caught some gray fox as well as skunk, 'possum, and 'coon. Only a couple badgers were trapped that season. They never shot trapped foxes. Bill would tap them on the nose to stun them, and then remove them from the trap and stomp on their heart area behind their front legs, to kill them. Don preferred to break their necks after stunning them. With both methods, there was no blood around the sets. Skunks were a different matter. If Bill wanted to release one, alive, he showed Don how to do it without getting sprayed. This method will be described in another chapter of this book. If they were to keep a skunk for its fur, they shot it with their pistols, but all the blood and musk was gathered up and buried away from the set.

Bill hated feral cats and when they caught one, it was shot and used for bait. For lures, they used mostly "Super Call" and "Sierra Call" call lures along with gland lure and plenty of fox urine at each set. Bill taught Don to use a good "gob" of call lure or "plenty" of a liquid-type lure. Call lures were applied near the set, but out of reach of the animals and upwind from the set which in IA, was a northwest wind.

Trapped animals were carried out, whole, either in their packs or over their shoulders. Don said that one morning they trapped 16 foxes, so you can imagine what a load that was for each of them to carry 8 foxes back to the car.

After returning home in the evenings, the trapped animals were dropped off at Forrest Rider's place since he had a heated garage he let them use to skin and put up furs. When they arrived home, Edith had supper ready for them, and they always had plenty of good food after a long day on the trapline. After supper, they would return to Forrest's garage to skin, flesh, and stretch the pelts of the day. Don would do the skinning and wash dirty pelts, if necessary, and Bill would do the fleshing and stretching. Forrest was sometimes there, and he and Bill visited and passed the "frostbite lotion", back and forth, while Bill worked. After the pelts were dry, they were moved upstairs to a loft and stored until they were sold. Bill instructed Don how to remove glands and parts from skinned animals to be used in his animal lures. The carcasses were then thrown into a barrel to be picked up by a rendering company truck. It was usually after 10 PM, and sometimes after midnight, when the fur work was completed, and they would head back to Bill's house to bathe and go to bed. That year, Don stayed at the Nelson's in the upstairs bedroom. He would go to bed, but Bill would stay up to fill lure/bait orders and to answer correspondence. Don said he would fall asleep to the "pecking" of Bill's typewriter and it might be 1:00-2:00 AM before Bill finally went to bed. Although Bill could operate day after day with little sleep, Don said he was hard to wake up and he insisted that Don wake him up at 4:00 AM, regardless of how little sleep he had received.

No matter how bad the weather was, Bill insisted they check traps, every day. The only exception that Don could remember was when it was so cold, the fuel line froze. They had to have the car towed back to town and put inside the service station to thaw out. In spite of that, "Bill didn't fret," Don said.

Don recalled some memorable days and numbers. One day, they trapped 7 foxes out of 8 sets and the 8th set had been visited. Their best set location produced 14 foxes that season.

They pulled up their traps after a month of trapping and ended up with 195 fox, 146 reds and 49 grays. They also lost 27 more foxes to thieves.

When it came time to sell their furs, Bill took them and went, alone, to the fur buyer. Don stayed home and sorted and cleaned traps and equipment. Fur prices were very low and in an article he wrote several years later, Bill stated they had only received an average of $.70 each for those 195 fox pelts.

After that season, Bill was interviewed by the "DES MOINES REGISTER" newspaper and an article appeared on January 9, 1949. Don was kind enough to provide me with a copy of it.

Bill had a policy of not trapping the same area two years in a row, so the next season of 1949-50, he and Don operated in Decatur County, about 100 miles west of Farmington. They rented a couple cabins in the little town of Leon, to operate from. Bill drove his Kaiser car that season with the same amount of speed and daring as he did with Don's car, the year before. This area had a few coyotes and Bill insisted on using long wooden stakes on all their traps. Don said they used mostly "Lobo Lure" and "Wolfers Pack" call lures when making coyote sets. Bill told Don his favorite coyote lure was "Lobo Lure". He also told Don not to use "Algonquian" call lure when there were a lot of 'coons around, as it was very attractive to them.

Bill with a coyote trapped in Decatur County, IA during the 1949-50 season.
(Photo by and courtesy of Don Paul)

Don said Bill would return home to Farmington every weekend to fill lure orders and answer correspondence, but he always returned late Sunday night and was ready to hit the trapline, early the next morning.

Since they had not had time to do any preseason work and the weather was very adverse that season, they ended up with a rather disappointing catch of about half from the year before, plus a few nice coyotes.

Before season ended, Bill had asked Don if he would be interested in trapping the big tidewater mink along the feeder creeks and rivers on the CA coast, the next year. Don was agreeable to this and they tentatively planned to do it, but later that summer, Bill drove to Don's home and regretfully informed him they would have to cancel the trip. So, that was the last year that Don trapped with Bill, as he entered into a new career.

Bill continued trapping with student-partners into the mid- 1950s, even though fur prices remained low. He wrote, *"Since my return from the CA country, my trapping has been a sort of 'hop-skip' prospecting variety that could almost be termed 'rocking-chair' trapping, as I most certainly have not put in a full-fledged season of steel-stringing since the season of 1945-46 . . . Since my* return, I have run sort of a prospect line each season in a different area. All told, I have covered and sampled 6 or 7 counties. Most all of this trapping has been rather high-speed work on fox, with an eye ever-cocked toward a possible future 'big-time' water line. Trapping seasons have varied from 30 to near 60 days. Much of it being late starts in new areas, with no valuable preseason work being done." He went on to describe the low fur prices he had received. "... I managed to pile up enough long-haired furs to make it interesting ... Rather than haul fox to my favorite fox buyer, I unloaded them to a local man. They moved at a flat $.90, with no throw-outs or poor #2s. This resulted in a grade price equal to $1.25 for #1s and good #2s. Even coyotes sold. 'Possums sold at $.40-.50 if skinned and stretched, civet cats moved at $1 flat, and my last batch of 'coons sold for $5 .... "

Bill with part of the 1949-50 catch he made with Don Paul that included a few coyotes they trapped in Decatur County, IA. (Photo by and courtesy of Don Paul)

When trapping season was over, Bill would take it easy, at least by his standards, and catch up on work he had put off such as making lures, writing articles, answering correspondence, submitting ads, and preparing for spring and summer work. During 1955, he released his first book, THE NELSON SYSTEM FOR THE WATER TRAPPER followed by his second book, THE NELSON SYSTEM FOR THE COYOTE-WOLF-BOBCAT-FOX AND COUGAR TRAPPER, in 1957.

It was very obvious that it was very hard to make a living during those years from fur trapping, alone, and without his lure business, giving instructions, wildcrafting, writing articles, selling his books, etc., Bill would probably not have survived.

Chapter 8

AGGRESSIVE ADVERTISING

Bill began an aggressive advertising campaign in 1946 to promote his dirt antifreeze method, lure formulas, instructions, and eventually his lures. His ads appeared in FUR-FISH-GAME, THE TRAPPER'S WORLD, THE NATIONAL TRAPPER'S DIGEST, TRAPPER'S LIFE, TRAPPER AND SPORTSMAN, and several other smaller and obscure magazines, from then until the late 1960s. He employed partial and full-page ads as well as classified ads. He was not afraid to spend money for advertising and sometimes, a single issue contained a full-page, a partial-page, and several classified ads. His ads were boldly-worded and often contained eye-catching claims, customer testimonials, and photos. After a few years in the business, some of his ads claimed he had boxes of testimonial letters from customers that he would gladly show to anyone who wanted to see them. Compared to other ads from his competitors at that time, Bill's ads were more bold and "wordy" than most. I'm sure some of the other lure makers and trapping instructors were somewhat intimidated, if not disgusted, with his ads, but I do not recall ever seeing any public written complaints or rebuttals in their ads, however.

I have often wondered how many trappers actually took up his offer to examine the customer testimonials he had. Once while visiting him and Edith, he gave me a couple of boxes full of old black and white photos to look through while he was typing some correspondence, upstairs in his office. I spent at least an hour looking through the photos and he would occasionally pause from his typing to explain a photo and where it had been taken, etc. I never asked to see any testimonial letters and he never offered to show them to me, either.

On the following pages are his various ads that appeared over the years.

This was probably Bill's first magazine ad that appeared in October 1935.

Attention Trappers—Get my master trapping methods and make your traplines pay. Years of actual experience and successful trapping is back of these methods. You will never regret your investment. Scent formulas and other valuable information free with methods. Write for prices. Bill Nelson, R-1, Box-21, Bigfork, Minn. (10-12)

Attention All Trappers! For the first time Bill Nelson is releasing his animal lure formulas to other trappers. Nelson has spent over twenty years in extensive lure making research and experimenting. Hundreds of dollars have gone into these experiments, and the resulting scents have been developed and perfected along traplines throughout the mid-west, the north, the west and the west coast. His reputation as a widely experienced trapper and fur taker stands back of every one of these deadly formulas. Now is the time to make and age your own dope. If interested write to Nelson for full information and prices. Bill Nelson, Farmington, Iowa.

Bill's first ad for his lure formulas appeared on August 1946.

NOW IS THE TIME TRAPPERS

ake up your own lure :pply now so that it will be roperly aged and blended. /ith Nelson's Superior Animal Lure Formulas you will e able to make up a superior lure that has no equal. o black magic or super-ystery material, no imposible claims. These formulas re the real trapline article eveloped and proven by one f America's most widely experienced trappers, and uner every actual trapline ondition known to man. hey are for trappers that ant a "dope" that really orks.

hese are not a list of old re formulas that have been ating around. They are the xact formulas used by a ian that does not need to egin earning a reputation s a fur taker; he earned hat years ago. These are the real articles for real trappers, developed by a veteran in this rapping game. If you are really interested in lures that truly call furbearers write for full iformation and prices.

BILL NELSON, FARMINGTON, IOWA

FOR THE FIRST TIME TRAPPERS . . . .
NELSON'S SUPERIOR ANIMAL LURE FORMULAS

are being released to other trappers. Here are formulas that have been developed by one of America's most widely experienced trappers. Over twenty years of very extensive experiments and careful testing have gone into their development, as well as hundreds of dollars expended during that time.

Nelson developed and perfected these lures, not in one "back pasture" or one localized trapping area, but along very extensive traplines throughout the mid-West, West, North Woods, far-West and West-Coastal sections. There is no haphazard brews or book-borrowed bunk in these formulas. He has developed, tested and proven the calling power of these lures while trapping for the fur animals that he is offering formulas for. It is not a case of a fox man offering a formula for marten and fisher, or a 'rat specialist offering information for making dopes to take such animals as wolf, coyote and bobcat. These are dopes that have been used by a seasoned trapper that has trapped for the animals along extremely long traplines, and under every trapline condition known to trappers.

Nelson invites any man to investigate his reputation as a fur taker in any section in which he has operated. He is offering no "trash," but invaluable information to trappers that wish to make up, or have made up, good "dopes" that will really call the furbearers that they are intended for.

Not a single one of his formulas have the power to do impossible things, but each of them will allow you to make up some of the surest and deadliest animal lures that have ever gone into a bottle.

If you are interested, write for full information and prices.

BILL NELSON
FARMINGTON, IOWA

When answering ads please mention The Wildcrafters World

FOX AND COYOTE TRAPPERS . . .

The Nelson Cold Weather System will mean dozens of extra fox and coyote at a time when other trappers take but few animals. Not an outline of trap settings, but a booklet crammed with condensed fur-taking secrets that mean success. Includes the only 100% effective antifreeze method I have ever tested or used. Keeps a damp dirt hole set working in twenty below. Use at any dirt set for any animal. Includes the secrets of PROPERLY scenting the dirt hole; how to keep them "alive" and attractive; the truth about no-fear; a cold-weather bait that WORKS; a call lure that has no equal, and how to use it; both valuable formulas. Other tricks. Not the writings of a beginner, nor a new over-night expert. This is fur taking information written by a veteran fur taker with a reputation open to any man's inspection. This system worth real money and very cheap to use. Price, $8.00.

BILL NELSON, FARMINGTON, IOWA

Bill released his dirt antifreeze method in April 1947.

Nelson Trapline Photo. Iowa trapline, ten below zero, dirt catch.

NELSON'S SUPERIOR ANIMAL LURES
FOR
The Fur-Taking Trapper

The Nelson's Superior Animal Lures are being released this season in limited quantities. About half of them will have to be withheld until mid-winter or this spring. These are real fur-taking lures, that have been developed, tested and proven along long traplines through many states and sections. They are the lures developed by one of America's best known and most widely experienced trappers. No super-mystery or black magic material; but real down-to-earth, fur taking lures that will do what the buyer can rightfully expect of a lure that he has paid out good money for. Give them a trial and you will never use another type of lure, and you will quickly agree that they are unlike anything you have ever before used.

Call lures for coyote, wolf, bobcat, cougar, red and gray fox, mink, 'coon.

Gland lures for bobcat, mink, red fox, Matrix lure for red fox.

A Food-Gland lure for gray fox that is also a top coyote lure.

Fall and Winter lure for muskrat. All lures $1.00 per ounce, with 10% discount on lots above $20.00.

I can also supply properly handled red fox urine, 90% female at $3.00 per pint, $5.00 per quart, $18.00 per gallon.

Finest lure ingredients that money can buy. No cheap compounds or solvent weakened material. Prices on request.

BILL NELSON
FARMINGTON, IOWA

When answering ads please mention The Wilcrafters World.

Bill began selling his lures in 1947.

BILL NELSON, FARMINGTON, IA.

NELSON'S SUPERIOR ANIMAL LURES

$1.00 per ounce

THE LURE SUPREME FOR FUR TAKING TRAPPERS

20-oz. or more 10% Discount

THE GREATEST TIME TESTED AND TRAPLINE PROVEN LURES EVER DEVELOPED

Available at last in limited quantities, the Nelson Superior Animal Lures. Here are heavy, full bodied lures on which no expense has been spared. Properly based and fixed lures for the fur taking trapper. Over twenty years of very extensive lure experimenting before being released. Lure experiments conducted along very long and active traplines throughout the West, Mid-West, North, Far-West and West Coastal regions. Lures that have stood the acid test under every trapline condition known to man; farmland, North Woods, deserts, rain drenched coast, high, Alpine regions. Developed and perfected by one of America's most widely experienced and well known veteran trappers, the Dean of All-Around-Trappers.

Gland Lures for Red and Gray Fox, Bobcat, Mink—Special Call Lures for 'Coon, Fox, Coyote, Wolf, Bobcat, Lynx, Cougar, Mink—Matrix for Fox—Fall, Winter and Spring Lure for Muskrat.

Here are lures that are different than anything you have ever used before. If you use them as I direct you will increase your fur take and you are going to agree that they are the deadliest "dopes" ever crammed in a bottle. Used correctly, by experienced or careful trappers these lures will do what trappers have expected of commercial lures, and more. These are not black-magic concoctions for which I claim impossible things. They are, instead, the real down-to-earth trapping article that you trappers have long looked for. Give these lures a fair and honest trial along your traplines, and if you do not agree that they are the best you have ever used, return the unused portions and I will cheerfully refund your money.

I have tested hundreds of lure formulas, developed and tested dozens and dozens of my own. Being an active professional trapper operating along all types of traplines and under every kind of terrain, cover and climatic conditions I needed real lures, attractive to the animals I trapped for. I have those lures, and they are being made available to you now.

Write for price lists on Lures, Baits and the Finest Lure Ingredients in America.

I more than welcome tests made against any existing lures.

Use the Nelson Cold-Weather System and stretch Fox and Coyote when the other trappers' stretcher supply gathers dust.

See my other display and classified ads in this issue.

BILL NELSON, FARMINGTON, IOWA

NELSON'S SUPERIOR ANIMAL LURES

Superior Lures
Made By A Trapper
For Trappers

The Lure Supreme for Fur
Taking Trappers
$1.00 Per Oz.
20-oz. or more 10% Discount

TRAPLINE
PROVEN

Call Type Lures

Super Call: The King of the fox calls. Also a fine coyote lure.
Wolfer's Pack: A proven killer for any member of the wolf clan.
Pacific Call: Special experiments over a twelve-year period to develop this 'Cat Lure. At last a lure that really pulls the cold nosed 'cats. For bobcat, cougar, lynx. Fine for "spooky" coyotes and wolf.
Gland Gall: The deadliest 'coon lure ever crammed in a bottle. Bear, too.
Ambra-Musk: A new and different type of mink lure, and a money-maker.
Muskrat Lure: A proven taker for fall and winter use. Powerful.
Musquash Oil: An extremely powerful and attractive 'rat lure that has no equal. Tops in any area and any season.
Muskrat Special: A top lure for spring use. Also for heavy trapped areas during the mid-season. Strong food element lure.

Gland Type Lures

Red Fox: A powerful gland lure that really "foxes" a set.
Gray Fox—Food, Gland: A fine lure for the sharp-nosed grays. Also fine for reds and coyote.
Matrix Lure: A very powerful matrix item for the reds during late winter and early spring. Also attractive to grays.
Muskall: A gland lure for mink. This has been a proven killer for over twenty years. Far reaching and long lasting.
Coyote Gland Lure: Here is a real item for the Wolfer. A gland type lure that is different. Keeps the gray fellows working.
Bobcat Gland Lure: Very powerful and fine at any set alone or with a call lure.
Lure Ingredients: Top quality that has been trapline proven. I handle no half strength tinctures or solvent weakened materials. My prices are in line with the quality of the ingredient. Prices on request.

The Nelson's Superior Lures are the real down-to-earth trapping articles. Developed and perfected by a recognized veteran in this trapping game; a fur taker with a long standing reputation. No haphazard brews; no black magic; no super-mystery; no impossible claims. Just good, honest lures that do what a lure should do, or your money back.

Marten lures made on order. Beaver lure for spring release.

I welcome any and all fair trapline tests.

Mention this magazine when writing or placing orders.

Use the Nelson Cold Weather System and stretch fox and coyote when the other trapper has idle stretchers.

See my other display and classified ads in this issue.

BILL NELSON   FARMINGTON, IOWA

NELSON'S SUPERIOR ANIMAL LURES

Superior Lures Made By A Trapper For Trappers

The Choice of the Fur Taking Trapper, $1.00 per oz.
20-oz. or more 10% Discount

TRAPLINE PROVEN

CALL TYPE LURES

SUPER CALL: The real King of the fox calls. Also a fine coyote lure.

WOLFER'S PACK: A proven killer for any member of the wolf clan.

PACIFIC CALL: Here is a 'cat lure that really attracts the cold nosed cats. It has nothing in common with the usual type of 'cat lure. This is a real killer for bobcat, cougar and lynx. Fine, too, for "spooky" coyotes.

GLANDGALL: The deadliest 'coon lure ever crammed in a bottle. Tops for bear, too.

AMBRA-MUSK: A new and vastly different type of mink lure. A real money maker. Give it a fair trial and you will never again be without it.

MUSKRAT LURE: A proven taker for fall and early winter. A real food lure.

MUSQUASH OIL: There has never been a 'rat attractor like this, and it will never have an equal. A top lure for any area or in any season. Extremely attractive.

MUSKRAT SPECIAL: A top lure for spring 'rat trapping in any section, but a proven caller in any season. Fine in the marshes.

SABLE OIL: Here is a marten lure that definitely attracts marten. It has hundreds of marten to its credit, and is fine for ringtails.

NELSON'S ONE-ELEVEN DECOY: The master lure of all time for coyote, and extremely attractive to fox and wolf. Is recommended only to professional fox and coyote men. (See classified section on 1-11.) Priced at **$2.00** per ounce, with no discount.

SIERRA CALL: A wonderful call lure with a very high value for use at key sations in group trap settings. A special for bobcat and coyotes, but a real fox taker, too. Price: 1-oz. **$1.50.**

VALBARCH: A proven attractor for beaver in any area or season.

SKUNK AND 'POSSUM LURE: A very powerful lure that will increase your take of these animals.

GLAND TYPE LURES

RED FOX: A very powerful and heavy gland lure; one that really "foxes" a set.

RED FOX, MATRIX LURE: A powerful and different matrix item. Like my gland lure, it is very heavy.

GRAY FOX: A fine lure in areas where no red fox are to be found.

MUSKALL: A gland lure for mink that has been assisting in placing mink furs on the boards for over twenty years. A real lure.

COYOTE: Here is a real gland item that old and experienced Wolfer's will know is "made right" at the first whiff. Very dense and strong. A heap of "coyote taking" back of this dope.

BOBCAT: A fine gland lure to use alone or in connection with "calls" for the bobcat.

NOTE . . . With the exception of the Sierra Call and the 1-11 Decoy, all lures are priced as indicated at the top of this ad. I make special prices on coyote gland lure to professional wolfer's that use a lot of gland lure alone and in connection with call type lures.

Remember, Nelson's lures are trapline proven items developed by a veteran in the trapping game with a reputation as a fur taker. I do not make haphazard brews, nor do I have any black-magic dopes. I do not deal in Super-Mystery, nor do I made impossible claims. But I do sell lures that truly call the animal, or animals, they are intended for. If it is really strong testimonials and references that you want, just let me know and I will supply them. And remember, the first and the twenty-first bottle of lure you buy from me are the same, and a lure purchased this season will be the same fur-taking dope when ordered five years from now.

See my other display ad and classified ads in this issue . . . and mention TRAPPERS WORLD when writing or ordering lures.

BILL NELSON -:- -:- **Farmington, Iowa**

Trappers -- Predator Control Men.......

GIVE THE NELSON'S SUPERIOR ANIMAL LURES A FAIR TRIAL ALONG YOUR TRAPLINES AND LEARN WHY A FAST-GROWING ARMY OF TRAPPERS ARE USING THEM. A two weeks test and I am confident that you will join my listed group of "REPEAT CUSTOMERS".

No man has carried on more extensive, and expensive, lure experiments than I have. I have trapped and worked with lures along large traplines throughout the North Woods; the Mid-West; West; Far West and West Coastal regions. I have trapped and worked with lures in every known cover and climatic condition. I have trapped every known furbearer and have earned a "fur-taking" reputation that I am proud of, and I did not earn it with articles telling the trapping fraternity that I was the BEST at the game, or that I had set any RECORDS. I earned it taking fur through the farmlands; the North Woods; the deserts and the big waters; the big sticks and the big bush and along vast mountain ranges, and I have done it along the coasts. From over twenty years of this kind of trapline work and trapline lure experimenting, the Nelson's Lures were created. Today, I welcome tests made against any existing lure.

With the exception of two; I have satisfied customers in every state, throughout Canada and Alaska. Hundreds and hundreds of America's top fur trappers use my dopes. Dozens and dozens of America's really "top-flight" Wolfers and predator control men use my dopes by ounces and pints. You simply have to have something better than good to please these veterans of the traplines.

And, what I have said for my lures, I say for any printed material I offer for sale. And what I have said, I will back with references that mean something. And if it is testimonials that a serious trapper wants; he can have them by letting me know and paying postage and registered mail fees on original letters . . . or he is more than welcome to visit me here and learn at first hand.

Today I give personal instructions to both young trappers and veteran trappers from Iowa; Missouri; Illinois; Indiana; Ohio; Wisconsin; Minnesota; Michigan; California. At this writing I have additional reservations made from most of the above states, plus Colorado. I have stacks of inquiries from many other states. There must be a very good reason for that, too.

There are some good reasons . . . I sell animal lures that are deep bodied; far reaching; long lasting and attractive to the extreme. I deal in trapping information that is "fur-taking" information. The simple and deadly systems and methods that bring results.

BILL NELSON -:- **FARMINGTON, IOWA**

Several of Bill's classified ads clumped together for the photo. Sometimes, one to four ads appeared in a single issue.

NELSONS SUPERIOR ANIMAL LURES

Fur-taking lures that have been, and are, making trapline history. Aci tested under every existing climatic condition and in all sections of th U. S., Canada and parts of Alaska. Used in every state in the Unio1 Here are lures THAT ARE PREFERED BY THE FUR TAKIN(TRAPPERS OF NORTH AMERICA. Dopes that have proven thei merit to the old timer and beginner alike, used by predator control me throughout the great Western, North and South-Western areas; alway gaining in its enviable reputation.

Not only do our leading trappers depend on Nelson lures, but they us the Nelson trapline system and methods in hundreds and hundreds c cases. I teach trapping here in the field on special appointments and als

type up instructions on request. have trained many, many trapper from Iowa, Ill., Mo., Ind., Ohio, Ala Colo., Mich., Minn., N. York, Wis. N. Jersey, Wash., S. Dakota, N Dakota, Penna., Nebraska, Canada

I have no "bargain counter" lure for sale. Some are costly .. BUT . they produce results. They are crammed to the muzzle with the world's costliest ingredients, skill fully blended and aged. Made fron Nelson's own rare and unusual form ulas. Formulas backed by near thirty years of extensive trapline experi ments and costly testing. Backed and made by a man with a well know1 and well earned reputation as a fur taker. A reputation earned alonj long traplines in Mid-West, North, West, Far-West and West Coasta areas.

You get full value for the dollars invested in my lures and instructions Boxes and boxes of testimonials prove that.

WRITE FOR LISTS AND LITERATURE

Bill Nelson, Farmington, Iowa

FUR TAKERS, BOUNTY COLLECTORS:

Trappers throughout North America agree that the Nelson Superior Animal Lures are the deadliest animal attractors that have ever been made available to trappers. Here are lures that have made some fur taking history that is a matter of record. Lures made by a recognized authority on trapping and by a man that is a known veteran of the fur trails. Nelson's lures are unlike any dopes ever placed on the market; each one is a lure that is constructed from Nelson's rare and unusual formulas that are a strict departure from any and all accepted theories of lure construction. Many Nelson Lures are costly, but each and every one represents the soundest investment that a fur and bounty collector can make. I extend an open invitation to anyone to read the boxes and boxes of testimonial letters that are here on file. Letters you would have to read to believe. Nelson has also instructed an army of trappers from over half the states of the Union and sections of Canada. Every Nelson student is a finished fur taker. His reputation as a trapper-instructor is without parallel. Following are a few excerpts from letters such as I receive throughout each new year. "Your Super Call is something, got 82 fox in ten days". M. P., New York. "Started this season with 11 different mink lures, over 70% of my mink caught with your Ambra-Musk". B.W. Vermont.

SIX OF A KIND TAKEN ON THE TAIL OF A HIGH SIERRA STORM.

"Your mink scent is more than you claimed; the best I ever used". G.F., Wisconsin. "Your system of set location alone was worth more than the price of your instructions". R.V., Ohio. "Tried your gang system and got twenty fox in four days at two locations".F.V.H. Michigan. "I sure found out that you taught me more than I ever dreamed of". P.L., Michigan. "This is the only lure I have ever used that really gets the mink". H.R., Ohio. "Your muskrat lure simply amazing. Took 130 with one ounce". C.R., Virginia. "Received the instructions and they could not be beat; if a person cannot catch his share of foxes with your help he better give up trapping for good". C.W., Wisconsin. "Again I say your scent is tops. In fact, it is too good as a man could exterminate bobcats in an area in a short time with it". A.W., Calif. "Would like to say here and now that your lures are the best on the market". L.V.W., Iowa. "Your mink lure really works, and I have tried a lot of them". J.W.C., Penna. "Your Ambra-Musk and Muskall are truly wonderful lures". A.K.A., Washington. "Take this opportunity to tell you that your lures are the best I have ever used". C.L.V., Missouri. I could go on for many, many pages. These few excerpts give you a small idea, and all original letters on file with hundreds of others. Write for literature and lists.

BILL NELSON   FARMINGTON, IOWA

TRAPPERS

Nelson's Superior Animal Lures are a standing challenge to any dopes ever poured into a bottle. Test them against any existing lures and then you be the judge. I have no sales bargains, no three for two and a half sales specials in lures that cost me far more than that to make ... BUT, I do have dopes that will, and do, produce fur-taking results that are more than amazing. Boxes and boxes of testimonial letters here on file that I challenge anyone to equal, and these are open to public inspection and reading by ANYONE.

Jim Burns of Grant City, Missouri graphically illustrates the results that are obtained with the Nelson's Superior Animal Lures.

Nelson's ability as a fur taker, a qualified instructor and a maker of animal lures that have, and continue to, make trapline history is a matter of national record. If it is references that are in order I am ready, willing and able to supply them. A scrap book as thick as your arm is open to inspection. I refer you to Editors of leading papers, magazines, Fish and Wildlife and Conservation officers, U. S. Forestry Service, ranchers, trappers and outdoorsmen throughout the U. S.

In the future I will begin to display letter excerpts from the countless letters I have here on file, and I will continue to do so, month by month and year by year. All of them backed by originals here on file, and ones that I am most willing to allow you, and you, to read. Many, and many, that I would not dare allow to appear in print ..... BUT, you can read 'em just anytime you drop by.

A great army of the nations greatest fur-takers use Nelson Lures by ounces and by pints. These are men that do not throw away dollars, but insist upon a return for money invested, and they get it when they invest in my dopes ... and this is attested to through the fact that my business is based upon an ever expanding "repeat-order" sales return through customers that are not only satisfied, but willing to pay far more than prices quoted to obtain the lures that have proved to be indispensable in their business of fur taking and bounty collecting.

All this, and the fact that I have instructed a great army of trappers, beginners and veterans alike, from a total of 23 states and sections of Canada. Their success, too, is a matter of record.

Write today for lists and literature. Visit me and learn the facts for yourself that are here for reading.

Bill Nelson, Farmington, Iowa

The beginning of a fur take along a Nelson trapline.

NELSON'S LURES

These Superior lures have made, and continue to make, a heap of fur taking history. Used by an army of satisfied customers throughout North America. Developed and perfected by a man that most certainly needs no introduction to the trapping public; a man that has gained a well earned and enviable reputation as a fur and predator taker and one that is Nationally known as a qualified authority on wildlife and as a trapping instructor with the ability to instruct and improve the trapline knowledge of beginner and veteran alike. My references are Fish & Game Commissions and personnel, U.S. Forest Service, ranchers, farmers, editors, newsmen and outdoorsmen. An army of lure customers and ex-students attest to the quality of the Nelson's Superior Lures and to the undeniable values of an instructor style that teaches a man how to take fur with systems and method applications that are fast, simple and deadly to the very extreme. Boxes of testimonial letters are here on file; many of them far too strong to ever appear in a printed publication, but they are open to your inspection at any time. I am ready, willing and able to prove any and all statements that I make. If you have never used the Nelson lures, you owe it to yourself to test them fairly along your own traplines. Each and every one a standing challenge to any dope ever poured into a bottle. All are compounded from the Nelson formulas that are a strict departure from any existing and accepted methods of lure making. They are truly different. Write for lists and literature.

BILL NELSON

FARMINGTON   **IOWA**

One of many thousands that have been taken with Nelson's Lures.

FOX-COYOTE-CAT TRAPPERS

Prepare now to get your share of those bounty checks. Such authenic records as the following are samples of what can be done with Nelson's Superior Lures and the Nelson System of trapping. Without even an all-out effort; 179 fox in 31 days, plus 37 stolen; 167 in 28 days; 195 in 30 days; 225 in 33 days; 21 fox from one set in 28 days; 7 fox from a group setting of 7 traps; 16 fox one morning; 21 fox one day and many equal fox takes. Up to 9 coyotes in one morning; 45 bobcats with an actual 36 settings during some part time prospect trapping, and this from a restricted area.

Trappers have made unbelievable catches of fox, coyote and 'cats with Nelson's Lures, and a small army of trappers have been instructed by Nelson from a total of 25 states and Canadian areas. These men have plenty to say about the Nelson system of fur and bounty taking, and a vast army of trappers have as much to say about the undeniable and deadly attraction that every bottle of Nelson Lures hold. Stacks and stacks of testimonial letters here for the reading at any time. I welcome and encourage their being read. My ads are based upon facts; not just drum beating and wishful thinking. Write for lists and literature.

BILL NELSON FARMINGTON, IOWA

One of Bill's ads that revealed some of his record fur catches.

TRAPPING

WATER TRAPPERS: Nelson's new book, "The Nelson System For The Water Trapper" is the greatest bit of fur taking information ever placed in print. Unlike anything that has ever been offered to trappers. This is a carefully detailed outline of the Nelson system for taking mink, otter, beaver, coon and muskrat. The chapters on mink and otter alone are worth a hundred dollars to any fur taker. The contents of this book has sold freely for years under my confidential instruction service for a total of $90. Is not a book of posed pictures, nor is it a brag book. It is simply an outline of fur taking instructions that are deadly to the very extreme. Written by a man that indeed needs no introduction to the trapping public. From boxes and boxes of testimonial letters here on file (all open to public inspection at any time) are a few excerpts. "I have your book on water trapping and think it is the best book ever written on trapping Mink and other water animals".M.F.K.,Penna. "Let me thank you for the book. It is everything you say, and without a doubt the finest book on the subject I've seen".I.L.,Ill. "I have been studying your system for the water trapper and think it is the best buy I ever made".J.B., N.Y.: "Your wife talked me into one of your water books. Thought it would be the same as some of the other books I bought. How foolish; it is far Superior and sure has increased my knowledge".LRMS.,Penna: "Received the Mink book (Water System) and found it to be just as I knew it would be; darn good. If anyone can't catch mink after studying-that, they had better sell their traps".B.W.,Vt. "I have been told of your wonderful book on water Trapping. With this fellows success with your methods, I believe you are one of the best".B.S.,New York "Got your book on water trapping. Must say it is worth every cent of the $5. Have trapped mink 25 years, never seen nor heard of some of your mink sets".R.W.,Minn. These are samples such as I receive from all sections of the country each week. For something that is really new, and vastly different, order your copy today. Price $5. Bill Nelson, Farmington, Iowa.

FOX, Coyote, Wolf, Cat Trappers: Nelson's reputation as a fur taker and predator trapper is nationally known, and is based upon something far more solid than copy-tha-other fellow-methods, drum beating and wishful thinking. He has instructed an army of trappers from what is now a total of 25 states and sections of Canada. All his students meet with top success, and many have earned enviable reputations as fur takers and bounty collectors. He deals in no super-mystery, no trick sets, no wind blown magic; just simple and extremely deadly method application and trapline systems. Confidential typed instruction service, or personal field instructions on appointments. Write for literature and prices now. Investigate, too, the booklet that covers the only 100% efficient system for handling dirt sets in snow and far below zero weather. This booklet under copyright in 1947, & today portions of it have become the most plagiarized bits of trapping information ever placed in print. Not only have many plagiarized portions of its contents, but have even commercialized upon some of the very cheap materials that the booklet directs to use. For the complete system as published by Nelson, order your copy today, "The Dirt Set In Freezing Weather & Cold Weather Tricks". Priced at $5. Bill Nelson, Farmington, Iowa. JA7

FOX----PREDATOR TRAPPERS

"THE NELSON SYSTEM FOR THE COYOTE-WOLF-BOBCAT-FOX & COUGAR TRAPPER"
Priced at $10.00

Since the days of the thirties I have received a steadily growing request from trappers for a book covering my system for fox and predators. The past fifteen years this request has grown. You asked for it; here it is, a complete and detailed coverage of the Nelson System. The coverage on fox alone is worth many, many times the price of the book. This is a book of advanced instructions that is vastly unlike anything you have ever before read. Every word contributes to a system of fur and bounty taking that is fast, simple, deadly efficient. It does, I assure you, strip all the "frills" and the "fancies" from this type of trapping. Once and for all time it de-bunks the "bunk". It places right things in their right place, and it eliminates all the complicated, time consuming trap-trickery and super mystery material that has been thrown your way for all too long.
IN THIS book, chips lay where they fall, as it teaches you the many "little tricks" of the game that are so very important. Nelson's ability and reputation as a trapper is one that certainly needs no airing here. He is Nationally known in the field, and his reputation as a trapper-instructor is without parallel. Every fragment of worth-while trapping knowledge he has learned down through the years is presented in this great book. It is outlined in an easy-to-understand style that will give you the greatest return you have ever had from a trapline investment.

BILL NELSON, FARMINGTON, IOWA

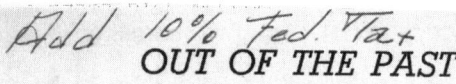

OUT OF THE PAST

Add 10% Fed. Tax

An ancient art revived! The ancient Indian's "lost" art of making his weapon points has envolved into beautiful and exquisite jewelry.

Through an exclusive process, a combination of ancient and modern methods, these very unusual pieces are offered. Each arrowhead specimen a beautiful duplication of the highly desirable "Columbia Gem Point" Arrow.

STYLES

ARROWHEAD EARRINGS	Dangles Clip-Ons Pierced	Pair—$2.00
ARROWHEAD NECKLACES	18 inch Gold Plated Chain	$2.00
ARROWHEAD BOLO TIE	On fine 18 inch Braid	$2.00

Available in the Arrowhead colors of Agate, Obsidian and Jade.
Dealers Prices Upon Request.

MRS. BILL NELSON, Farmington, Iowa

Edith had her own ad, too, for her hand-made arrowhead jewelry.

Chapter 9

THE FISHERMAN

Bill loved to fish, and learned how when he was a kid. No matter where he was at, if there was fishing available, he was there. From the rivers and creeks in IA, to the rivers and lakes in MN, from the coastal feeder rivers to the high mountain lakes and streams in CA, and to the frozen lakes in MT, he fished them all. He not only enjoyed fishing, he was good at it. Good enough that he guided other fishermen, at times.

CATFISHING

"Many of my happiest memories are associated with days and nights spent along the big, lazy rivers of the Midwest; learning their secrets and moods, and from kid days until now, every-trying to take more and bigger, catfish. Taking freely, too, from the thousand-and-one sights and sounds that are so indelibly a part of Old Man River."

Bill fished all types of catfish in his section of IA: channels, blues, Fultons, and flatheads. He stated the favorite foods of most catfish were small mussels and water snails, but they also fed on crawfish, minnows, hellgrammites, stone and mayfly larvae, caddis cases, and worms. Also, grasshoppers, when they were out. Sometimes, wild grapes and mulberries that fell into the water from overhanging vines and branches. He even caught catfish on kernels of corn.

Although some paste baits worked well for him, some of the commercially-available ones he tried were worthless. Same with ones he made from the $1.00 formulas that were readily available. When using cut baits, he liked chunks of white-fleshed fish such as shad, quillback, suckers, and gar. He also liked sun-weathered liver dipped in his fish lure oil.

He mentioned catching the biggest channels during the spring flood periods in June-July below drifts, fallen trees, below points of land jutting into the water, small bays, and the intersection of streams. During the time they were migrating, he like to use minnows and small sunfish or bluegills, 2-to-2-1/2" long, hooked into the dorsal fin. As the rivers subsided, crawfish and hellgrammites worked well for him.

Although channel catfish are more active throughout the day than most of the other catfish, he still liked to catch them at night, from 10 PM until 4 AM. *"I like to sit by a big fire on the river bank and watch the shadows out on Old Man River. I like to listen to the music of the riffles, the splash of feeding fish, maybe the yap of a fox back in the hills, or the warbling cry of a 'coon among the cottonwoods and willows. When the moon peeks out and makes the riffles and shallows look all silvery, the river really becomes a thing of beauty. Soon, the stars show up, thicker and thicker, you breathe the cool, fresh air and you wonder why the dickens you don't do more of this night fishing than you do. Or, if you have never done it before, why the duce you haven't?"*

For day-fishing, he recommended fishing the deep holes in dark waters along rock ledges and drifts. He said rocky-bottomed sections of river were especially good.

For blues, he liked to use small live sunfish, minnows, and frogs early in the season and hellgrammites and clam baits, late in the season.

He called Fulton catfish the *"gray ghost"* and said it took extended periods of high water to start them moving upstream. He told of the flood of 1947 that was the worst in a century, flooding many of the towns along the Des Moines River and driving people from their homes for days on end. This happened, twice, within days of each other. This flood brought the *"vanguard"* of the big catfish runs, however. He said Fultons hug the banks while scouring them for crawfish, frogs, and nymphs. In slick water, they feed on minnows, bullheads, sunfish, and bluegills. When resting, they seek out quiet pools below drifts, small bank bays, eddies below fallen trees, and at the mouths of small streams. For fishing Fultons, he recommended live sunfish or bluegills, 3-5" long, hooked through the back, just under and to the rear of the dorsal fin. Large-sized Kirby-pattern hooks worked the best, but he cautioned not to use too hard or too tempered hooks. He used

2-3 hooks per line on stagings 10-12" long and weighed down with window-sash weights. He also cautioned against spacing the stashings too far apart because baits would be too far up in the water. He liked back lines that were 15-20' long and attached large barrel swivels on the hooks.

Bill said flatheads had a ravenous appetite and would go for all the baits previously mentioned, plus *"freak"* baits like rotted eggs, sparrows, and baby chicks. When using live baits, he recommended they be 3-6" long. Even big gobs of worms the size of a tennis ball would work, he said.

For set lines, he liked to use a heavy twisted cotton-cord line for throw lines, the length depended on how far he thought he could throw them. A slightly smaller line was used for stagings, or strips, and they were 12-16" long and to which the hooks were tied. The stagings were tied to the throw line 2-3' apart. Twelve-to-fifteen stagings were used per line. For hooks, he liked the bronzed Limerick hooks in sizes 1, 2-0, and 3-0. He stressed keeping the hooks sharp at all times with a small pocket sharpening stone.

For trot-line fishing, he used a much heavier cord and spaced the 12-15 stagings 8-10' apart. When the rivers were high and muddy, he sometimes dropped a middle weight from a length of cord attached to the center of the trot line to hold the baited hooks down and also to steady the line.

Bill and Mutt with a couple of catfish ready for the frying pan.
(Photo courtesy of Marlene Rider)

He noted some big catfish being taken out of the Des Moines River over the years: a 51-pound flathead, several blues in the 30-pound range, and one giant over 50 pounds. An old-timer around Farmington told Bill that two men were hand-fishing and caught a 70-pounder, years before, and it took both of them to bring it in after a long, hard battle.

For eating, Bill preferred channel cats to any of the others, stating they would only be second to clear-water trout or walleyes. Right behind channels, he liked to eat Fultons. Flatheads and blues were farther down his list, but he ate them all.

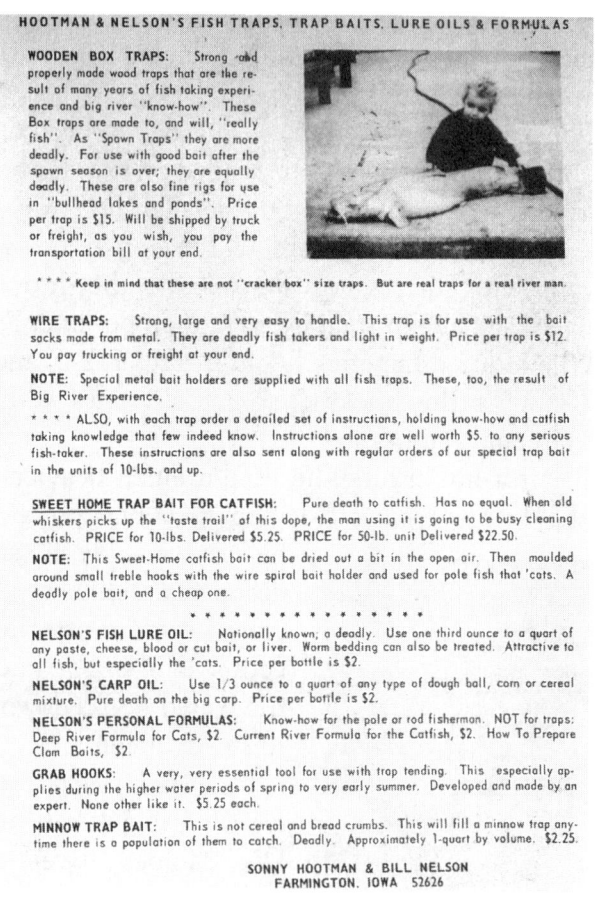

Bill's and Sonny Hootman's ad for catfish products.
This venture never materialized, however.
(Ad courtesy of Sonny Hootman)

Bill sold catfish bait and also a carp oil and fish lure oil. I do not believe these were a big part of his lure business, however. After his young friend, Sonny Hootman, got out of the Navy in 1960, he and Bill teamed up a few years later to start a fish trap, bait, and lure business, separate from Bill's animal lure business, but neither of them had sufficient capital to properly operate, advertise, and promote the business, so it never materialized. Years later, Sonny developed a catfish bait, himself, and put it on the market. Today, he is one of the most prominent catfish-bait manufacturers in the country and his "SONNY'S SUPER STICKY CATFISH BAIT" is tops. Bill would be proud of him.

While gathering information for this book and visiting with Fuller Laugeman, he told me that when he and Ruth had picked up the inventory of lures and ingredients from Edith after buying Bill's lure business, there were several cases of pint jars of "WILLIS NO FAIL CHANNEL CAT AND TROUT BAIT" in a shed. They did not know what Bill had used this fish bait for, or why he had such a large quantity of it. Fuller was kind enough to give me a few jars of this old bait. There was a phone number on the jar label, and I called the number to see if I could learn anything about the bait. An elderly man answered the phone and I told him who I was and why I was calling. He told me he had not heard from Bill in years and wondered what had happened to him. I explained to him that Bill had died many years ago and asked him why Bill had bought this bait. He told me that Bill told him he used it for animal baits and he sometimes bought it by the 5-gallon pail. I guess we'll never know exactly what Bill did with this other brand of fish bait. It's just another one of those secrets he took with him to the grave.

CARP FISHING

In many areas of the Midwest, carp are considered a trash fish and are not fished for food consumption. Bill stated he did not like to eat them but once or twice during the spring. He said the meat was too sweet and loud-smelling, for him.

He did have some advice for those who did fish for carp, however. He recommended using set lines in eddy waters or in water 3-6' deep, without much current. He stressed keeping the hooks on set lines near the bottom, since carp are, indeed, bottom feeders. For baits, he recommended worms or sweetcorn kernels during muddy, high-water periods and dough baits for low, clear water.

MUSKY FISHING

Bill had a special fondness for musky fishing. "*Musky fishing is unlike any other rod and reel sport. A musky is mean, a musky is a sulker and a flirt, a musky will never do the right thing at the right time. Now and then, it seems that a musky will be located that has to be wooed; you locate the rascal and then start a sort of solicitous courtship. You offer the red-eye old warrior every lure in the tackle box, you try every trick in the game, and when you reach the point when you are about to admit defeat, he swarms out of hiding and smashes that last offering with a fury that starts a thin path of goose flesh tracing way up your spine . . . A musky has every tackle-busting trick in the game, down pat. A bundle of neurotic temper that swaps ends under water and walks the full length of a pool on its tail. Here is a fish that can roll like a spinning log against a taunt line one second, and then suddenly tower out of the water with a head-shaking leap that shows the angry red flare of gills- just plain mean . . . All musky seem to be temperamental.*"

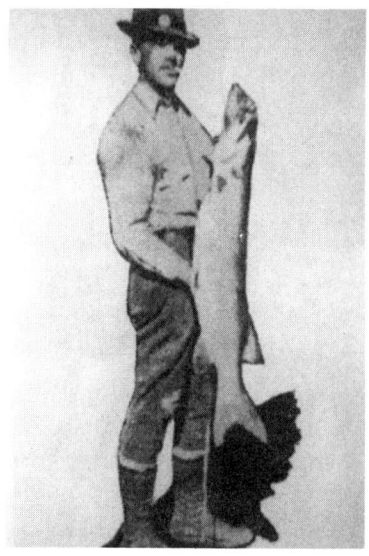 

Bill and Edith with muskies they each caught.
(Bill Nelson photos)

Bill said the two most important factors in successful musky fishing were patience and appreciation of the fish. His favorite method of fishing them was to spot them resting in the river and then offer them the lure. "*Many large musky are hermits. The finest art in the game is to know how and where to locate their hiding place. After a time, you learn to recognize favored hang-outs.*" For lures, he liked Pflueger Bearcat spinners with a medium-sized dipsey sinker and also, Pike-Orenos. He was most successful by dropping the lure about 6' ahead, and a little to one side, of the resting musky and using a slow retrieve.

Bill started fishing for muskies during the fall of 1934 in northern MN when he and a friend took a 6-day, 25-mile trip on the Bigfork River. They caught several muskies, two of which weighed 12 and 25 pounds, along with several walleyes. After that, he was hooked on musky fishing and made several more trips for them that year and in 1935. He became quite proficient at it and started guiding musky fishermen, as a source of income. He mentioned guiding a client from the Twin Cities for 5 days, and they caught their limit of 4 and released 8 smaller ones. "*You can't catch them all,*" he said.

TROUT FISHING IN THE SIERRAS

While living in the Sierra Nevadas of CA during the early 1940s, Bill fished the alpine lakes and streams for trout. He wrote an article about taking Edith with him to Gold Valley in early June. Since there were still snow banks on the road, they had to hike and climb 4-1/2 miles to the trout stream they wanted to fish. At the summit, they enjoyed the view and he pointed out numerous landmarks and lakes to her. Dropping into Gold Valley, they reached the stream and Bill showed her how to fly fish. They used #14 coachman flies with a small mosquito dropper on a 3-pound test line, as well as small badger-hair flies. By noon, Edith had caught 5 rainbows and he, fifteen. Stopping for lunch, he noted, "*As we sat there in the sun and watched a fluffy spray of white cumulus clouds float out over the valley sky, a great golden eagle passed overhead on silent motionless wings. Certainly, he added a touch of majesty to the templed hills around us."* After lunch they continued to fish and caught six more, including a brook trout that Edith landed.

The lake that fed the stream they were fishing was another 1-1/2 miles up, and Edith insisted they hike to it. *"As we neared the summit, purple dusk was settling along the valley below us and had started to steal up the mountain sides. The evening sun touched the lake briefly for us and then ducked beyond the ridge to the west. From the high ridge, we could again see the sun. It was a burnished red-gold disk resting on the rim of the distant coast range.*

Bill admiring a rainbow trout he caught in Gold Valley in the Sierras while fishing with Edith. (Bill Nelson photo)

By the time we reached the lower end of the valley, Edith was regretting those 3 extra miles of climbing . . . Then, darkness descended with that strange swiftness, so peculiar to high country.

Reaching the car, we loaded tackle and catch, then started the rough trip homeward, each silent with our thoughts of a day that had been rich with the better things in life."

Chapter 10

MONTANA PROSPECT LINE

In February 1955, Bill's friend and customer, "Cactus" Wade, urged him to come for a visit and do some prospect trapping for beaver in the Big Sky country of Montana. Because it had been 10 years since Bill and Edith had been in the West, they jumped at the chance to see new areas and Bill could do some aerial surveys of the country. They left the Minneapolis airport the first week of March and flew to Billings, MT where it was 8 below zero. There, they changed planes and flew to Bozeman where it was even colder at 20 below, and then on to Missoula, and finally to Kalispell, where they were met by Cactus and his wife, Win. They drove to Wade's 4-W Ranch which was along the Fisher River at the base of the Cabinet Mountains, between Kalispell and Libby. The Nelson's relaxed at the ranch for a couple weeks and Cactus showed Bill around that part of Montana and they enjoyed some ice fishing for silver salmon. Bill studied maps of the area and made notes for a potential future trapline. On March 29th, Cactus drove Bill to Great Falls via Missoula and Helena through more country that Bill had never seen. Bill was impressed by the vastness and rugged mountain ranges he saw. The next day, Bill chartered a plane out of Great Falls and flew the Smith River drainages, looking for beaver sign. He was disappointed to find these waters were too barren for good beaver populations. The second day, he flew the Missouri River south of Great Falls towards Cascade, Wolf Creek, and Holter Lake and then back up the Dearborn River canyon. There, he saw country he was sure over a hundred beavers could be trapped in one month. He also flew part of the Sun River and noted more good country, there. Returning to Great Falls, he was confident he had located enough country for him and Cactus to run a decent prospect line. The next day, they headed back to the 4-W by a different route through Choteau and Browning so Bill could see more new country. The water pump on Cactus' car broke in Browning, so they were delayed there for a couple hours while it was replaced. Heading over the pass towards Glacier Park, they encountered a blinding ground blizzard, and it took 2 hours to get through it. They finally arrived at the 4-W, glad to be home.

After preparing equipment, they loaded up traps, boat, and other gear and headed back to Great Falls, 2 days later. Another MT blizzard struck, and they were stranded in town for a few days since travel in any direction was impossible. After the storm broke, they headed for Cascade and established a base, there. They began to string their traplines on sections of the Missouri, Dearborn, Smith, and the Little and Big Belt Rivers. Access to these rivers was the biggest limiting factor, but they soon learned where the access points were. Bill did not describe their traplines much, but did say they trapped some huge old blanket and super blanket-sized beavers.

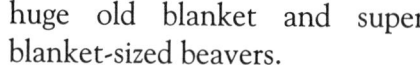

After a few weeks of trapping, Bill flew another prospect flight over tributaries of the Belts and into Logging Creek Canyon. He found even more good beaver country for them to trap. They continued to trap until the end of April and then pulled all their traps and returned to the 4-W. Bill summed up their prospect line as follows. "... *All in all, we covered a heap of country by car, plane, plane, boat, and on foot. We certainly lined up enough country to allow a couple of hard-working trappers to hang-up a most impressive beaver catch. This, of course, would take hard work and very serious trapping over a 2-month period. Many of the beavers we caught were true giants that were out of the blanket class. They were real super blankets. I personally saw no evidence of any real beaver trappers through the areas we trapped.*" Bill told Ron McIntosh they had trapped around 300 beavers on that trip.

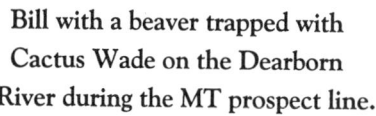

Bill with a beaver trapped with Cactus Wade on the Dearborn River during the MT prospect line. (Bill Nelson photo)

After cleaning, sorting, and putting away Cactus' traps and equipment, Bill relaxed a little and enjoyed their last few days in northwest MT. *". . . I took one last walk up through the pines and the larch that marched over the Cabinet foothills."*

After 64 days in MT, the Wade's took Bill and Edith to the train depot. *"We said our good-byes at Libby and boarded the Western Star that soon made its way up the twisting course of the river and over the Great Divide."*

This was not Bill's last trip to MT, however.

Chapter 11

BOUNTY TRAPPING

Since prices on long-haired furs were so low during the 1950s and 1960s, Bill depended on bounty money paid for predators which sometimes exceeded the fur price. He did not believe in the bounty system in itself as a wildlife management practice, but he did believe it was much better than having government trappers using poisons, cyanide guns, etc. He strongly opposed the use of any poison to kill predators and the secondary impact these poisons had on furbearers. Even though he opposed the bounty system, he was quick to "cash in" on them if they were paid in the area he was trapping. Sometimes, he trapped strictly for bounties, and other times he collected them while fur trapping. If he was bounty trapping before furs were prime, he wisely operated in areas away from his fur-trapping areas. Some years, he even went out of state to bounty trap. He especially liked northern MN since he had already trapped in, and knew the country around Grand Rapids, Big Fork, Big Falls, Little Falls, Loman, and International Falls. MN paid $5 on fox, $25 on coyotes, $35 on wolves, and $15 on bobcats.

In an article, Bill described an early-fall bounty line in northern MN with a partner, Joe, who was from WI. After arriving at their base location, they set up their tent and neatly arranged cots, stove, and food/utensil lockers. Bill was a stickler for a clean camp. "*To me, good food that is properly prepared, a good bed, and a neat and clean camp are important parts of trapping. I dislike poor food and I dislike dirt in any form.*" As usual, he did most of the cooking and mentioned he and his pard put away a lot of food at the end of each day. The tent was placed under some tall pines because Bill liked to fall asleep at night, listening to the wind blow through them.

They began to prospect and set traps along the way on September 17, 1958. They noticed more fox sign was present than when Bill had trapped the same area, several years before. But he noted fox would only contribute a small part of the total bounty take. Wolf sign was scattered and since wolves travel so much and for such long distances, he said it was hard to pin them down. He called them *"old bone crushers,"* referring to their huge teeth and powerful jaws that could crush moose bones and chew off 2"-thick limbs, when caught in a trap.

Even though the nights were frosty, mosquitoes would appear as soon as the sun warmed up the air. With disgust, Bill said, *"These rascals seem to be a sort of frost-resistant breed."*

Bill stated they usually made flat, scratch-up, and cache trap sets in the northern bush because soil conditions did not lend well to making proper dirt hole sets and also, there was another trapper operating along part of their lines who was using poorly-made dirt hole sets and they noticed coyotes had been digging up some of his sets.

Tent camp under the tall pines in northern MN while bounty trapping (Bill Nelson photo)

Bill on the bounty line in northern MN.
(Photo courtesy of Jack Harris)

After a week or so of trapping some predators, Bill and Joe headed for the county seat town and presented the scalps for bounty so they would have some operating money. Grouse and rabbit hunting seasons were open, and they stocked up on groceries that went well with the dinners of roast rabbit or grouse breasts that Bill prepared.

"We both like grouse and tonight, platters are heaped, high, with the browned white meat, well-seasoned with a touch of sauce, rosemary,

and sage. *Country-style fried potatoes on the side, bread and butter, fruit, and the coffee pot sending out its own special aroma. Ah, this is living, and the little stove spreads warm glow through the tent and outside."*

Bill noted they had problems with hunters stealing traps and animals and one day, they lost over $60 in bounty money to thieves. Bill hated thieves and once stated, *"Such lads need to have each ear notched with a chunk of lead so they may carry a sort of permanent identification mark. They need much worse, but I understand there is a law."* Don Paul related an incident where he and Bill came upon a thief who was messing with their traps across the river from them. Bill fired off a couple shots with his pistol in the vicinity of the thief who immediately fled and never bothered them, again.

Bears were another problem along the bounty lines. Although they could easily pull out of most #3 traps, a #4, 14, or 48 would often hold them, at least long enough where they would run off with the trap. As Bill put it, *"It is usually 'good-bye trap' at either staked or dragged settings."* Sometimes they could follow the drag trail and recover their trap, but more often than not, they never found it. He mentioned losing 3 traps to bears in one day.

3 coyotes and 3 foxes trapped on the bounty line. (Bill Nelson photo)

Bill noted that fishers had really made a comeback from previous years and said it was hard to release them from a trap since they fought it so hard and were either already dead, or injured so bad in the larger traps, they had to be dispatched.

Busy as they were, trapping, Bill and Joe sometimes took time to do a little fishing for a change of diet and they always enjoyed the crisp fall air. They also enjoyed watching pileated woodpeckers and other birds while checking their traps.

Bill enjoyed the nights in the north woods. "*Tonight, the mice are again playing on the tent roof. They run back and forth over the tent cloth, making a thin drumming sound as they go. Now and then there is a 'plop', as one scrambles up a guy rope and then leaps to the roof to start a new game. This game seems to occur mostly during nights when we have the little sportsman stove burning in the tent. Perhaps its glow and the warmth on the cloth attracts them. It is a friendly sound . . . Both the horned and the barred owls send their cries through the aisles of the forest . . . There is a great silvery moon above the dark forests of spruce that sweeps northward from our camp into Canada. The night is very quiet . . . ."* It was not always quiet, though. He related an incident where a skunk had waddled into their tent one night and while sniffing around, woke them up. Bill let out a yell. "*For a time, things were a bit tense as the battle flag was erected. However, he soon swaggered out.*"

On October 1st, it snowed, and it stayed on the ground. On the morning of the 5th, it was 15 above and the ice was thick in their water bucket. They continued to trap until the middle of the month, and then pulled their traps and headed back to IA. Bill summarized their bounty trapping venture. "*. . . We have seen a heap of country and had some nice hunting and eaten a heap of grouse and done a little fishing. We pulled in some bounty critters that kept things interesting. I have had the pleasure of learning that the deer are still plentiful and that the fisher has made its comeback. I watched for the first snows of the season riding the storm winds over the dark spruce forests. I have looked at my rivers and lakes, and the crisp air was good to breath, and deep was our sleep there in the little camp under the pines, each night.*"

The bounty system in MN was discontinued a few years later in 1965, so Bill was forced out of an area that he loved so well and he had to seek bounty lines in others areas that still paid them.

Chapter 12

BACK TO MONTANA, BUT NOT FOR LONG

Bill tried out-of-state ventures in MT the next 2 seasons of 1959 and 1960, but circumstances beyond his control prevented him from fulfilling them. In 1959, he teamed up with Gus Gehlhar, a young trapper from CA, on a proposed all-out mink line in western MT. They arrived in East Helena early that fall and based there with the help of Bill's friend and dealer, Jack Harris. They began to prospect and map out their proposed trapline. Gus provided all the traps and equipment and was driving a 2-wheeled drive pickup. Mink season arrived in November, and Bill and Gus began to set out their lines. Without warning, an early blizzard hit and dumped 3' of snow and dropped temperatures to 30 below zero. Thinking it would pass in a few days, they waited and hoped for the best. Days turned into a week and after another week, they decided they had better dig out and salvage their traps while they could. Although they did recover some of them, they could not find many of them, and had to leave them for good. After 3 weeks, Bill knew when to cut his losses, and he and Gus headed back to IA to try and salvage a season, trapping fox. Gus said everything was frozen solid and they had to start from scratch, but they still managed to trap over 200 foxes that season.

The next fall of 1960, Bill returned to East Helena with a young man named Jim (Jack couldn't remember his last name). He was very inexperienced and it appeared to Jack that the trip was more of a vacation for Jim rather than an education on the working trapline with Bill. Bill later told Jack's wife that the trip turned out to be *"Much on the order of baby-sitting."* For whatever reason, Jim told Bill he could not continue to trap with him because of a "family emergency," so once again, Bill had to cut his losses and head back to IA and hit the fox lines, by himself.

As far as I could learn, this was the last time Bill was in MT or any other western state. From my visits with Bill and from talking to some of his friends, old partners, and associates after he died, it appeared that Bill pretty much stayed in Farmington throughout the following years tending his lure business, giving personal trapping instructions, writing articles, wildcrafting, and trapping with student partners. He did tell me that local farmers would come and get him when they were having problems with predators killing their livestock. He did not have a phone at that time, and he told Bill Waterman in a letter of March 10, 1969, "... *I would not have a phone in the house. Have not for 2 years. My years as a federal and state officer made me dislike phones. I still do . . . .*" He also quit driving sometime during that period. I heard several stories as to why, but could not confirm any of them. Most of the problems the farmers had were from coyotes, but Bill told me he sometimes trapped coydogs and rarely, red wolves. He charged $50 to trap the offending predator. He told me about a "large canid" that was killing pigs on a local farm. From the tracks he found, he guessed it was either a dog or a coydog. After setting some large traps for it, he first trapped a coyote, but the next trip around he had a 70-pound red wolf.

Bill also told me he would sometimes work for a roofing contractor at times when he needed extra money. This was mostly "hot tar" roofing on flat roofs and he described how hot and miserable it was, but that it was easy for him to get work because most men would not do it and he had a higher tolerance to heat than most men and the experience to readily get hired.

Chapter 13

THE HUNTER

Bill Nelson was not a well-known hunter who wrote articles about his experiences as many other outdoor writers of his era did. Instead, he could be classified as a sport and subsistence hunter who hunted because he enjoyed it and to put meat on the table. He learned to hunt squirrels at an early age. *". . . Then, too, the squirrel rifle would be lifted from the pegs in the kitchen. Happy days in the hickory groves. Early mornings spent Indian-hunting those that chattered and gave away their location. Later in the day, drowsing beneath a den tree, waiting for a saucy gray to expose itself, or waiting beneath the larger hickories for the tell-tale sound of a nut being gnawed, or the sounds of one being dropped trough the leaves by a careless fox squirrel. Ammunition was hard to get at that time. Money was none too plentiful. I learned to ease out my breath and squeeze the trigger of that little Remington with loving care. Seems now that it had a special little snap all of its own, and the sound of the squirrel tumbling down through the branches and thudding among the fall leaves. And the smell, too, of powder smoke on the fall air."* He also wrote, "I perhaps like squirrel hunting better than anything the outdoors can offer, other than the actual trapline, itself."

Bill was a crack shot with a pistol. Here's 2 squirrels he bagged with it. (Bill Nelson photo)

He was a deadly shot with a pistol and often hunted squirrels with one, only taking head shots. Don Paul described how Bill showed him how to shoot a pistol from a sitting position for more accuracy. He would sit with both knees drawn towards his body and with both hands gripping the pistol and elbows resting on his knees, he would draw a steady and accurate bead on the target. For shooting squirrels higher up in the trees, he would plant the soles of his feet against the tree trunk and draw his knees up higher to achieve the proper support.

I already mentioned him harvesting rabbits and grouse for meals while bounty trapping in northern MN. Marlene Rider told me that Bill and Forrest Rider used to like to hunt pheasants, together, and Bill mentioned in an article how good the pheasant hunting was in southern MN when he was there in the 1930s. He once told me he had *"camp meat,"* no matter where he was.

John Barbee said Bill had shown him some of the guns he owned when he visited him, one time. Among them, was a Model 25 Remington slide-action carbine, an L.C. Smith double-barrel 12-gauge shotgun, and a Stevens Hi-Standard 22 pistol. Bill wrote of using a 25-20 and a 32-20 to kill bears and deer when he was in CA. Jack Harris told me Bill had bought a new Savage Model 99 .358 Winchester caliber rifle that fall he and Gus were in MT with the intention of hunting moose and bear, but he never got the chance to use it.

Bill's long-time buddy, Forrest Rider, with some pheasants they bagged. (Photo courtesy of Marlene Rider)

Don Paul traded a .38 Colt automatic pistol to Bill for that L.C. Smith double-barrel 12-gauge shotgun while he was trapping with Bill. He kept it all these years until 2 years ago when he presented it to me as a gift. This is one of my most prized possessions in my collection of Bill Nelson memorabilia and I will be ever grateful to Don for this special gift.

Bill got a taste of cougar hunting with hounds that fall of 1959 he was at East Helena, MT. He told Jack Harris he would like to go on a hunt, so Jack loaded up his hounds and they drove into the foothills to see if they could find fresh cougar tracks. It was 30 below zero and windy, and not fun to be out in. They found fresh tracks in the snow, and Jack turned the hounds loose on them. He and Bill strapped on snowshoes and took off, following the dogs. After an hour or so of trudging through the snow and bucking the cold wind, Bill persuaded Jack to end the chase and turn around and head back to the truck. Evidently, being somewhat out of shape and reliving the cold and hard times of years past, got to Bill.

Chapter 14

THE TRAPPER

"... To the man that has never followed the trails of the traplines, I can only say, 'You have missed much'... You will find him rich in health, happiness, and the things of life that are most worthwhile, and mellow with the memories of a life well spent in God's great, clean outdoors... Ah, for the life of a millionaire, say some- but just let me stay a trapper."

Although Bill liked to be referred to as an outdoorsman, he was probably best known as a trapper. This is not surprising, as his books and the majority of his articles were about trapping. Remember, too, his boyhood dreams which were mostly about trapping. During his lifetime, he trapped over 20 types of furbearers and predators: striped skunk, spotted skunk (civet cat), 'possum, 'coon, red fox, gray fox, mink, muskrat, weasel, coyote, gray wolf, red wolf, coy-dog and other hybrids, bobcat, fisher, marten, bear, badger, cougar, ringtail, beaver and otter. There may have been more, but this is what I counted up from his writings. A pretty impressive resume. I once asked Bill if he had ever used snares or deadfalls to catch animals. He mumbled something about *"That was what Indians used, etc...,"* and I got the message.

Since Bill's two trapping books and his dirt antifreeze method are still available, I am not going to repeat the sets he used, his set location descriptions, etc., but rather review some of the information he provided in his articles that weren't necessarily in his books and are so vital to the success of trapping the animal he writes about. He referred to some of this information as the *"little things or tricks"* and said they were just as important as the sets that one used. I will also reveal some of the record catches he made and some weights of animals that he recorded.

FOX TRAPPING

Years ago, Bill noted there was a lot of controversy around the country as to who was the best fox trapper. His answer to that was, *"There will never be a best fox trapper, or any other trapper."* He stated several times throughout the years that some of the best trappers in the country were not in print and were unknown to most trappers, and that's the way they wanted it. He told me his best fox catch was 427 in one season. He told Ron McIntosh the following season he trapped 367. These were tremendous catches in those days, considering how much walking he did to tend his traplines and were done without the use of 4-wheeled drive vehicles, ATVs, snowmobiles, etc. In those years, catching 100 foxes in a season was considered a big catch. More of his record catches were already revealed in the advertising chapter. He once told me that catching 50 foxes in one area might be a better indication of a trappers ability than catching 300 in another area. He warned me not to get too hung up on numbers and their indication of a "good" or "poor" trapper.

After returning from CA in 1946 and trapping fox in several counties for a number of years, he wrote that he had trapped over 1,000 foxes from those areas, with at least 100 of them being stolen. One year, he lost 37 foxes in 31 days to thieves, but managed to pelt 179 during that time. Besides what he trapped, he knew of over 300 more that were taken in the same areas by other trappers and hunters. Although he stated that fox were able to sustain heavy harvests year after year, he believed in giving areas like this a rest, every few years, just to ensure adequate populations.

Here's the "old master" making a fox set on his trapline in IA. (Bill Nelson photos)

During the late 1940s and early 1950s, Bill wrote that a trapper could make good money at that time if he could average $3.50 per fox on an average season's catch. Otherwise, one would have to catch more fox at lower prices to make it worthwhile, or operate in areas where there were bounties.

When trapping fox in IA, he wrote in would catch 20-25 gray foxes for every 100 foxes he trapped. Therefore, 75-80 would be red foxes. After weighing scores of foxes, he said grays would weigh 9-10 pounds on average, with some going 11-12, 13, and a few rare heavy ones at 14. He didn't mention average red fox weights, but did say he had trapped some unusually heavy ones weighing 14, 15, and 16 pounds.

He reported that most of the Townsend gray fox he trapped in CA were very calm and did not offer to lunge or bite at him, when trapped. In fact, he would sometimes pick up some of them in his arms after releasing them from the trap and carry them off to free them. If they started to struggle, he would lightly slap them with his hand and they would curl up and close their eyes, similar to 'possum behavior.

MINK TRAPPING

Bill had a real fondness for trapping mink that started with his boyhood. He wrote, *"For a few years, a trap to me was simply something that you set for a mink. I got so I thought only in the terms of a mink."* I already mentioned that Bill would insist on making a few mink sets while trapping fox, no matter how busy he was.

Bill advocated preseason scouting for mink during late September and early October. He said females would often raise their litters at the headwaters of small streams and dry ditches and bucks could often be found in these areas, too, during the early part of trapping season. He recommended trapping those areas first, because a lot of trappers wouldn't consider trapping them, and then move to the larger creeks and rivers after the weather got cold and the big bank-runner mink showed up.

Although he said it was encouraging to see mink sign when setting traps for them, he said trappers should set traps at good locations whether they saw sign, or not. He stated he had probably seen sign of only a fraction of the mink he had trapped.

Bill liked to trap mink in MN. Here he is prospecting, there.
(Bill Nelson photo)

Bill said many trappers set too many traps at one stop or section for mink. He said 1-3 was plenty at any one stop. Normally, he would pull them up after the 3rd or 4th check on his 2-3 day traplines and move them to new country. He was confident he could catch the majority of mink, by then. He stressed speed and efficiency when trapping mink. He considered trappers who walked up and down creeks for hundreds of yards looking for perfect blind sets to be wasting their time and by-passing good locations where man-made sets could quickly and easily be made and then move on to the next bridge. On the other hand, he criticized *"stab trappers"* who *"stabbed"* a trap into every hole and crevice they came to. He did use blind sets, but only if they were available when he wanted to make a set.

He did not use many baits during the early part of the season, since mink food was generally abundant. He waited until cold weather arrived and ice began to form on the waterways. He always covered his baits, even at pocket sets. He used lure at almost all of his sets, even blind and bait sets. He stated that proper use of good mink lures would probably increase one's mink catch by 40-50%.

He used dry sets when they were appropriately located, but mentioned they would undoubtedly catch skunks, 'possums, civet cats, weasels, etc.

Bill really liked to trap mink in MN and listed it as one of the top mink-producing states, both in fur quality and numbers, but he warned that freeze-ups came early and only trappers that knew how to properly make dry and snow sets would continue to make good catches long after the *"fair-weather"* trappers had pulled up their traps for the season.

COYOTE TRAPPING

"The coyote cry, for some reason, never fails to get under my skin. It makes my heart beat a little faster, and every time I hear it, I find myself holding my breath until the last quavering high notes fade away. It is sort of a trapline tonic . . . You see, I sort of like coyotes. Sure, I like to trap them and I know as well as you that they must be controlled. But, I like to see it done decently, and not at the cost of other untold wildlife . . . I feel that coyotes are as much a part of America as tall corn, fat cows, juke boxes, and fast cars . . . old smarty, himself . . . prime prince of elusive trap-dodge cunning . . . living symbol of our great outdoors . . . Let us hope that at least a few will always be around to serenade us around the campfire."

Bill didn't recommend anything smaller than a #3 double longspring trap when trapping coyotes and he preferred the Newhouse brand. He realized they were too expensive for most trappers, but he liked the quality of them and said they would stand up to the beating a coyote would give them better than other brands of traps. For larger mountain coyotes and for snow trapping, he recommended #4s. He did not like jump or underspring traps of any kind for trapping coyotes.

Bill liked to use a variety of sets when trapping coyotes. He noted some coyote trappers didn't like, or wouldn't use dirt hole sets. He answered, *"The dirt hole, made right and lured right, and placed in the right place, will take coyotes in any state in the Union . . . However do not depend on them 100%. Use an equal number of flat sets, scratch-ups, cache sets, etc."* He also mentioned coyotes had a habit of looking most everything over with care, before approaching it. As to their sometimes overrated intelligence, he stated, *"Coyotes are not the extremely cunning critter that most give him credit for being. But, on the other hand, he is certainly not a dumb animal and actually does possess a bit more than his share of natural wild cunning. I simply want to by-pass all this mythical and almost-intelligent bunk. Any trapper with* experience or training can outwit any blasted coyote that ever drew breath, and make no mistake about that."

Bill stress simplicity. ". . . Coyote taking must be kept simple unless the trapper wishes to have his trapping efforts turn into an outdoor school for educating coyotes . . . It must be kept simple in order to operate with a system that allows speed-trapping and the land coverage that is so necessary to big coyote taking."

He noted that coyotes travel a lot and may stay in an area for a few days and nights and then move on to another area, not returning to the first area for 3-10 days.

Bill sometimes threw out little tips without fully explaining them. A couple are as follows. "Badgers and coyotes have something in common. Learn that fact and never forget it" and, "A trapped coyote often howls while in the trap. Smart coyote men make use of that fact, too."

A nice day's catch of 6 coyotes and 1 bobcat. (Bill Nelson photo)

Bill related a story to me where he was trapping coyotes in a pasture where there were some horses. One morning, he checked his traps and found one of them had been pulled out of the ground, stake and all, and there was no evidence he had caught a coyote. He thought maybe someone had found the trap and stolen it, but he didn't notice any man tracks, either. Puzzled, he checked his other sets and started walking back to the car. He happened to walk by those horses and noticed one of them was dragging something from its mouth. He walked over to it and found the #3 Newhouse clamped onto its lower lip. After some *"excitement,"* he released the horse from the trap. He said this was the *"biggest"* catch he had ever made in a trap. I told him he ought to start selling horse lures, and he really laughed at that.

Bill recorded the weights of coyotes he had trapped over the years, in various states. In MN they ranged from 27-45 pounds, in IA, 21-34 pounds, in CA, 23-32 pounds, desert coyotes, 21-26 pounds, and mountain coyotes, 24-40 pounds. I don't recall him mentioning or writing about any season-catch totals on coyotes, but he did mention trapping 9 in one morning, in one of his ads.

BOBCAT TRAPPING

"After a great many years of trapping which has been spent along every known type of trapline and in pursuit of every known furbearer, I still find the wildcat or bobcat the most interesting furbearer that walks. He is also perhaps, the most cussed and discussed animal that exists, with the possible exception of the coyote. Personally, I have spent more time studying this bewhiskered outlaw than I have spent on all other animals, combined . . . Down through the years, I have written many articles on 'cats. Perhaps because this animal holds a sort of fascination for me. I just plain love to trap 'cats and have been very successful at it."

Bill with 2 bobcats trapped on the bounty line in northern MN.
(Bill Nelson photo)

Bill stated he had trapped hundreds of bobcats and traveled a few thousand miles in the process. He told me his best season's catch was 125. His biggest piece of advice for successfully trapping 'cats (and cougar) was a system that combined both nose and eye appeal. He quickly learned that on his first cat lines in northern MN during the 1930s. He used whole-carcass decoys of 'cat, coyote, skunk, and mink. He also used red flags, rabbit skins, and whole birds as visual attractors. He learned in a hurry that 'cats were NOT cold nosed, as was commonly thought. He learned by trial and error that single odors such as beaver castor, skunk essence, fish oil, muskrat musk, and catnip oil were NOT as attractive by themselves as they were said to be.

As with most species he trapped, Bill preferred to stake his 'cat traps rather than use drags. He believed the trapped animal left valuable nose and eye appeal after being caught and noted catching 4-6 'cats from a single set, several times. During a prospect line in CA, he ran 36 traps for 3 weeks and trapped 35 'cats and lost 7 more for a total of 42. When using cubby sets, he used whole carcasses rather than small baits.

Over the years, Bill trapped several subspecies of 'cats including 4 within the West and one in the Midwest. He noted the best 'cat of them all was the pallid 'cat from the Sierra Nevadas in CA. He described them as very soft and silky-furred and they varied in color from a creamy gray to a rich blue gray.

Bill mentioned trapping several 'cats that weighed in the 24-26 pound class. The largest one he trapped in MN weighed 39 pounds; in Humboldt Country, CA, 28-1/4 pounds; and in Mendicino County, CA, 30 pounds.

OTTER TRAPPING

"Every time I see fresh otter sign along the waterways, I have a new case of otter fever."

Bill considered otters as a fine "extra" while trapping other water animals. He never specialized on them. When looking for sign, he said to watch for bank slides, piles of droppings, piles of undigested fish, and fish bones. He noted that some otters cover a large territory and will cut cross-country across land to reach other bodies of water and they could take days to come back.

He stressed simplicity when making otter sets and advocated using lures. He sometimes made artificial otters slides or go-back trails to catch them rather than spend a lot of time looking for natural slides and trails, as he did for mink.

WOLF TRAPPING

"The true timber wolf is a symbol of our last northwoods area ... Once you have followed the trail of the wolves, something happens to you. You develop a sort of hunger for the 'hunt' that is hard to shake off. You might well manage to follow general traplines on a very large scale and take well more than your due share of furs; perhaps, even a good run on the otter or 'cats; perhaps a fine spring run on the beaver waters or a season up in the alpine country on the trail of the marten; a small mountain of bountied and pelted fox may dull the edge, too, but never quite make you forget the thrill of the wolf howl."

Bill admired the timber wolf more than any living wild creature. He described the first time he heard a wolf howl at night while he was musky fishing in northern MN in 1934. *"It was the grandest, the wildest, and the most wonderful night sound on earth ... Prickles walked up my spine to the base of my head and then back down, again. I think I even stopped breathing, listening for and hoping to hear that howl, again. I did, three more times . . . ."*

Since wolves travel so far and take so long to return to an area, Bill had some advice for locating them. *"Locating a group in an area is half the job. My best trick in that department is looking for their kills and traveling country from sunset until 10 PM and listening for their howls."*

Bill thought the timber wolf was the smartest animal that roamed the woods. He claimed they could show almost-human intelligence and reasoning powers and would by-pass a lot of sets that used dead baits or prepared scents. For those wolves, only blind sets or scents using the glands or urine of other wolves from a different area might work. He preferred larger #14 or #48 Newhouse traps for trapping wolves, but noted their high cost was too much for most trappers. He said the only *"poor man's trap,"* then, was the #14 Victor jump trap with toothed-jaws, but he recommended using 2 of them at a set and using heavy drags with plenty of chain to hold the largest of wolves.

Bill never told me how many wolves he had trapped in a season of fur or bounty work, but he did write that he had caught 5 in a row on an old road, once. He "gang-setted," or set several traps close together, when trapping wolves to provide the best chance in catching one or several when they passed through the area. In case of a nontarget catch, he would still have traps working when the wolves came.

Bill said most MN wolves would weight 60-80 pounds, but he did trap one that weighed 123 pounds and saw another that weighed 150 pounds. He thought these larger wolves were a different subspecies that had drifted in from other areas and they had been taken in the International Falls area and as far south as Craigville, Effie, Bigfork, and Deer River.

The first time I visited Bill and Edith during the fall of 1969, I noticed the big wolf pelt hanging on their living room wall. He didn't say too much about it except he could get over $100 for it at the New York fur sales. At a later visit, he confided with me that it was actually a red wolf that he had trapped, locally. I sure didn't know the difference. Years later, Sonny Hootman confirmed that it was a red wolf and said that Bill had trapped it on Coppers Creek, near Bonaparte, IA.

COUGAR TRAPPING

"Cougar trapping is a specialized art that must have your full attention. Most of the better fur areas are poor for cougar."

Bill sometimes referred to cougars as *"long tails."* He noted that many cougars were trapped, not hunted, and some of the best cougar trappers lived in CA, OR, WA, and ID and they were "not in print." Bill noted that cougars are a creature of habit. *". . . This animal will visit certain saddles and points at mountain passes as surely as the sun comes up and the sun goes down. However, as often as not, it takes a cougar from 20-26 days and sometimes 30, to make its rounds."* Because of this, he said cougar sets had to be operable at all times, no matter how long that was. As with wolves, he liked to use #14 and #48 Newhouse traps when trapping cougars.

While trapping in CA, Bill found some areas that abounded with cougars and mentioned finding "scrapes" and piles of droppings of the size that reminded him of bear droppings in huckleberry country. He always wanted to return to those areas and run a full-time cougar line. *"Some day, I hope to be able to spend a full 60 days in that one great cougar country I found. Sixty days with 50 special cougar sets. What a great and thrilling trapline that would be."* Unfortunately, he never got the chance to fulfill that dream.

After a lifetime of trapping, a long-time friend of Bill's asked him, "Bill, if you should suddenly become very rich, so rich that you would need never again try and make another dollar, would you still follow the trapline each fall and winter?" Bill quickly answered, *"I would follow the traplines, come what may, even if my riches were such as to make me a second Midas. My friend went on his way a very puzzled man, and mumbled something about me being buggy . . . ."*

DIRT ANTIFREEZE METHOD

Bill began selling his THE DIRT SET IN FREEZING WEATHER AND COLD WEATHER TRICKS FOR THE FOX AND COYOTE TRAPPER booklet in an April 1947 magazine ad. It sold for $8, contained 16 pages, and listed on the last page was, "copyright applied for." He later included the method in his 1957 predator trapping book. Both of these publications are still available. By the time his book was published, he complained the method had been plagarized by several other dealers and method sellers and others were actually selling the product as a *"secret antifreeze."* I do not recall him ever writing or saying that he, himself, had actually come up with the idea of using the product as a dirt antifreeze, and as with many good ideas that are developed by several people in different areas, it is the person that publishes or makes public the idea that usually gets the credit.

This method of keeping traps from freezing in dirt during freezing conditions is very effective to temperatures way below zero and a multitude of trappers, including myself, used it for decades. It does have a down side in the fact it corrodes traps if they aren't properly waxed and can leave a wet spot on the dirt over the trap if too much of the product is used or if it is not prepared according to his directions.

In his literature, Bill said, *"This method will allow any hustling trapper to add dozens of fox or coyote to his catch at a time when fur is full prime and when the average trapper is through for the season. It will work with a foot of snow on the ground. This is not just a pup catcher, as it will take the peg-legs and the old-timers as easily as the youngsters."*

Bill told me one year while trapping during mid-winter when the ground was frozen solid and the snow was deeper than normal, he used a long-handled broom to sweep snow off his sets, which was faster and left less sign than shoveling. Several people had seen him out in the pastures and fields, "sweeping snow with a broom" and they thought "Nelson had lost all his marbles."

Bill's dirt antifreeze method works. Here he is all bundled up in 10 below zero weather with 5 foxes from the first 7 sets by 10 AM. (Bill Nelson photo)

This dirt antifreeze method has largely been replaced by equally-as-effective products that are not as corrosive or by using dirt coatings that keep it from getting wet and freezing. Nevertheless, Bill's system of antifreezing dirt he introduced to the trapping public 57 years ago, should not be forgotten.

RELEASING SKUNKS FROM TRAPS, ALIVE, WITHOUT THEM SPRAYING AND WITHOUT USING IMMOBILIZATION CHEMICALS

The two seasons they trapped together, Bill told Don Paul if they caught nontarget animals out of season, they would turn them loose, and this included skunks. Don thought Bill was kidding about the skunk part, but he wasn't. The first skunk they caught before season, Bill told Don to *"watch closely,"* as the next one would be his. Bill turned it loose without getting sprayed, and they went on their way. A few days later, they trapped another skunk, and Bill looked at Don and told him to *"get at it."* Don said he successfully released it, but he was nervous the whole time and it took him quite a bit longer to do it than what Bill had done. Later, Bill told Don how he had nearly split his sides, laughing quietly, watching Don release that skunk.

Here then, is Bill's method of releasing skunks alive from traps without them spraying and without immobilization chemicals, as told by Don. Putting on leather chopper mittens, Bill would hold a wooden broomstick handle in one hand and slowly approach the trapped skunk and quietly talk to it. While approaching, he would wave the broomstick in a slow circle off to one side, to focus the skunk's attention to it. If the skunk raised its tail like it was going to spray, Bill would stop advancing and waving the handle, and just talk to the skunk. When it lowered its tail, Bill would resume talking and waving the handle, and ease towards it. When he was close enough, he would quickly rap the skunk on the tip of its nose with the handle to stun it. Then, he would quickly grab the skunk with mittened hands and fold its tail under it, compress the trap springs, remove the skunk, and toss it, head towards him, as far away as he could. As Bill put it, *"This method is not for the weak and faint-hearted."*

Chapter 15

TRAPPING SYSTEMS AND PHILOSOPHY

"The real assets to trapping ability is the ability to be able to really think and analyze . . . After all, complete knowledge of the many strange habits of our fur animals and predators is of extreme importance in making good catches. The 'little tricks' of the game are far more important than the actual construction of generally-known standard sets or methods. Method application becomes far more important than knowing the method, itself. Proper set location can, in many cases, be as important as the set, itself . . . nothing under the sun in the way of fur-taking can replace a good working knowledge of all these important factors. There are no magic sets, no trapline-wizardry, and no super-material that will do the impossible."

Bill encouraged more trappers to made studies of the animals along their traplines, as he had done. *"Personally, I do feel that the average trapper would obtain far more interest and education values from his traplines if he were to make more careful studies of the animals he traps. A careful recording of true weights and measurements, alone, would be of real interest. I started this hobby while still a very small lad . . . I feel that such observation and study gives one a greater appreciation for the traplines and the things that the outdoors offers. I also feel that added-knowledge of wildlife can make a good trapper, a better trapper. I will, at least, continue to study as I know that I have a lot of room for improvement. The more I learn, the more I realize how very little I know."* Very humbling words for a man with so much knowledge and experience.

Throughout the years, Bill wrote that trap sets were only as good as their location. In some of his articles and his predator trapping book, he referred to set locations as the *"brightest pebble on the beach,"* and stressed *"salient features"* and *"points of entry and exit."* He was adamant about this. *"A good set is one that is located near or on a salient feature that the thinking trapper knows will be visited by any traveling animal. When he selects a location for a set, he is asking himself why he is making the set. If he cannot come up with a good answer, he will not make it."*

For fox trapping, Bill advocated prebaiting sets. That is, choosing potential set locations 2-3 weeks before season and constructing sets without traps, just baiting and luring them. Then a week before season, checking all the sets and noting which ones had been visited. This gave the trapper a good indication of the numbers of foxes in the area and whether his set locations were on target. The foxes that visited the sets would probably return, but that time, a trap would be waiting for them.

Bill liked to keep all of his trap sets simple and quick to make, since time is money on the trapline. All the sets in his books are evidence of that. He described his sets in general. "... *With but a few rather outstanding exceptions, most of the methods that I use today are a sort of blending of the simple little kid-day trapping tricks with the methods and systems I have worked out through many years of fur taking. Today, I continue to work out variations of them and I continue to learn, believe me. Right here, I might go so far along this trend of thought as to say that I know many fair trappers today that would become very, very good trappers if they would but put their feet on the ground, get their head out of the clouds of complicated trickery, and start trapping fur instead of muddling around with a heap of damn-fool, hush-hush, trapline magic mystery . . . I have used many other types of sets, and many that I have never seen in print. Yet, somewhere along the lines, someone else has most certainly used these very sets in some form. Not a few times I have seen some new and super-duper set come out that I can well remember using many years ago. Any trapper with many years of experience has had the same experience at one time or another. On the other hand, new sets will come out that are actually simple variations of old-time sets that were in use, 30 years ago. They are simple and good sets and certainly do have their place along a busy trapper's lines. Quite often these variations, or new system of application, is a very real improvement that turns a fair set into a very good one. Then, there are other freakish and complicated, and trick sets that have come out that are nothing more or less than methods to obtain some poor trapper's hard- earned cash. There is no such thing as any fool-proof set, any tricky and time-consuming magic set that is worth a Tinker's Damn to any serious and busy trapper. Some of these children of the imagination are enough to make a man spit on his steel trap and throw it in the river."*

Bill used a lot of gang sets, or setting several traps close to one another in a small area, to capitalize on groups of animals traveling together, to allow for catching nontargets and still having traps available to catch the target, and the catching of one animal would attract others to the area.

Bill used a lot of gang sets. Here he is resetting traps after catching a double on foxes. (Photo courtesy of Marlene Rider)

Since Bill read and studied a lot, he picked up information from others that helped him develop his own methods and systems of trapping. When he was very young, an old veteran trapper offered him a bit of advice he never forgot, as evidenced in his trapping methods for almost every animal. "If I were to give a young trapper the best possible advice with one very short sentence, I would tell him to dig a hole." He was a good listener, and stated he could learn something from everyone, no matter how much experience they had. In his earlier years, he learned from the partners he trapped with. He wrote, *"A good trapper is willing to admit that he has much to learn. You can always learn . . . Among these trappers, I now and then find a man who does not quite know it all. It pleases me to know and meet trappers like that, as I feel on an even plane with them, knowing as I do, that I still have so very much to learn. I am always glad to get an honest tip and equally glad to pass one along to a really deserving trapper."* I can personally vouch for that as he passed on some very good tips to me during our visits.

Regarding trap-shy, or *"super-cunning"* animals, as he called them, he wrote, *"I have yet to work with any species of animal, or any one individual among them, that ever showed anything more than a normal wild animal precaution. You give* them what they want in the right place, avoid any of the tricky approaches to the job at hand, and you are going to get that animal. Please do not give me the old malarkey about any animal being able to think and to analyze a problem like a normally intelligent man."

I mentioned, before, that Bill said there was no, nor would there ever be, a "best" trapper. He went on to say, "I still feel that the rarest type of trapper is the man that is truly an expert at the game regardless of what animal he is after, be it mink, weasel, skunk, marten, or bobcat . . . Of course, one must keep in view of the fact that most all good trappers do make a rather high catch in any of the species of animals they might be trapping, so they usually travel or move to areas where they can do so." He continued, ". . . I believe that I have often mentioned the fact that the number of animals taken by a trapper in any one restricted area need not dictate the true trapping ability of any one trapper. Taking 10 mink in one area may quite well spell expert trapping as surely as taking 40, in another . . . The same holds true for coyote, fox, bobcat, or what have you . . . Years of experience, alone, does not in any way indicate a man's ability . . . I have seen trappers with many years of experience, and among them quite an army that I have instructed, that simply did not have the ability to become top men . . . Believe me, I know plenty of men that have trapped 20-40 years that have neither the gift nor above-average ability. And, I know some lads with but a few years of experience that do have it. So, let us not come up with that tiresome and worn-out poppy-cock about 30 or more years of experience being any sure criterion of any man's fur-taking ability. I agree that experience, with everything else being equal, is a most valuable asset. I know plenty of hard-heads that are simply so mentally inflexible that they will never be real trappers. Yet, these are often the ones that make the most noise about being the top man, the record man of all time, the man that learned it all, years ago, and the self-appointed authority that is the very image of complete and absolute perfection in all he does. And, in boredom, I might add."

All of Bill's old partners that I interviewed agreed that he was well organized and a stickler for detail. Harry Batten remarked that Bill was too fussy for him. Bill was systematic about operating a trapline and even his two books were entitled, "THE NELSON SYSTEM FOR . . . ."

Regardless of the species of animal he was trapping, Bill believed in using several lures and alternating them throughout his lines, and especially at groups of sets. "Right here, let me tell you that this rubbish about any ONE single lure or lure type doing the job is indeed rubbish. It takes a planned alternating of call-type lures and variations in set types to really clean house."

Having run several out-of-state prospect lines throughout his career, Bill reflected back on them and made some comments. "I am cursed, or maybe blessed, with a burning desire to explore new fur areas, see new country, and learn new trapline angles that one simply has to learn in any new fur region. Trapline prospecting is often uncertain in actual fur-shed rewards, but there is no uncertainty in final prospect values and it does, I assure you, give a rich return in worthwhile and unforgettable experiences, it teaches you dozens of new and valuable trapline tricks as you go along, and it adds to your store of wildlife knowledge. I believe, too, that it offers a fine guard against the many physical and mental rust spots that the passing years often bring. Three or four years of such operations in any state will allow one to return and harvest furs in a well-organized and big-time manner. To date, my worst trouble has been that I simply have a very hard time making myself return."

Bill always advocated trapping furbearers only when they were prime. He thought no season for furbearers should open before November 20th, at least in IA. He also criticized fish and game departments who opened hunting seasons for furbearers before trapping season. He was also critical about the lack of enforcement by the various departments to catch and prosecute trap and fur thieves.

Bill truly believed the only way to maintain fox and coyote populations at a balance that was compatable with good game management and farming and ranching activites was through the use of full-time professional trappers that would be paid either by decent salaries or through a combination of lucrative bounties and decent fur prices. He scoffed at the idea of extension systems that taught farmers and ranchers only how to make scent-post sets and use urine as lure. As already mentioned, he disdained the use of poisons to kill predators.

"Kill off a species and you unbalance nature. Kill off all the coyotes in the West and then sit back and listen to people howl for their return so they can get rid of the millions of jack rabbits that will take charge . . . The use of poison in any form by a man only proves to me that he is not a trapper enough to do it with traps. Poking cyanide guns into the ground hardly means that a man is qualified to bear the title of either trapper or wolfer. The fact has long been established that it takes a real wolfer and the steel trap to eliminate the 'killer coyote' and the 'killer wolf'." Bill was well familiar with the poisoning done in CA by the old U.S. Biological Survey and later by the U.S. Fish and Wildlife Service in MT. He wrote, "Please let it be understood that I am well aware of the commendable works of the Survey. That I realize they have an important mission in the heart of things. That I have a real respect for many of the men that are now with the Survey and also for those that were at one time with it . . . I have no personal grudge against any individual man employed by the Survey, but like many others, I do have something very akin to contempt for any medium that will foster the spreading of poison for any birds, game, or fur animals. It is, my friends, a very smelly practice. When I say, 'like many others,' I am referring to that vast army of men and women that are trappers, hunters, fishermen, nature lovers, and students of wildlife that believe in a sane and just conservation of our fur and game resources. All this, in view of the fact that poison-spreading is as unnecessary as it is destructive. This, after fully realizing that there is nothing that any man may say or write that will ever undo the waste and blight of Survey poison operations throughout the fur lands of the West." Jack Harris told me he had introduced Bill to the local government trapper around Helena, MT and that Bill had been cordial, but cool, towards him and avoided any conversations about poisons.

Bill's systems and philosophies were the basis for many of those, today, and they inspired scores of trappers for decades, some who went on to be noted trappers and authors, themselves. One can usually detect the "Nelson" influence in some of them, however, and the old saying, "Copies are the biggest complement to the original," sure applies, here. Ron McIntosh put it very well when he said, "Bill was way ahead of everyone else. It took until the fur boom of the 1970s for others to figure out what he had figured out in the 1940s and 1950s. His books are as relevant, now, as they were, then, and no one else was putting out that type of material, then."

Chapter 16

FUR HANDLING AND MARKETING

"An animal has only one pelt to give you, so the least you can do is treat it the best you can."

Bill wrote several articles on fur types, grades, and proper handling and marketing, over the years. He noted that St. Louis, MO was no longer the fur center of the U.S. that it had been since colonial times. New York was the new fur center.

Bill had some good advice for trappers on how to properly care for furs, once they had skinned them. *"After many years of trapline, fur-shed, and buyer-room observations, I am very much aware of the fact that most all furs are very, very poorly handled. If you are to realize good prices for these furs, you simply have to take care of them. So much of the 'coon, skunk, and 'possum fur I have seen has been very trashy. These are all fatty animals. They call for careful fleshing, wiping, and stretching. They should be kept wiped down after fleshing in order to avoid grease burn and dirty-looking pelts. After being removed from the fur forms, the fur sides should be well-combed towards the head to fluff up the fur and make it stand erect. All such furs should be well combed, free of burrs and all dirt, before stretching.*

After fluffing with combs, they can be further improved by snapping the dried pelt, carefully. This tends to make fur and guard hairs stand more erect. Foxes and coyotes can be further improved by beating, or flaying, the furs well with a long wooden paddle. After this process, comb the pelts from tail to head. Then snap the pelts, carefully, several times and hang on lines where the furs will not be pressed and crowded too much."

Bill recommended a small table fork for removing burrs and sticker followed by a large, strong comb. For fleshing, he liked a carpenter's draw knife and working the pelt from head to tail, wiping the pelt often with grease rags. He stressed that fleshing was shaving, not scraping. He also used a crescent-shaped butcher knife for fleshing. These are called "skinner" knives. He highly recommended the Herter's "Wilderness Crooked Knife." I bought several of these from Herter's before they went out of business and found them to be excellent, as he had said.

On fatty pelts, he recommended hanging up the pelts, fur side out, in a cool place for a day or two, to let the fat harden somewhat, which made them easier to flesh.

On "fancy" furs, furs that were skinned with the feet attached, he recommended a pair of hand pruning shears for clipping the toe joints from the foot pads.

For furs that were stretched pelt-side out, he liked one-piece solid fur forms. For furs that had to be turned fur-side out, he preferred two and three-pieced fur forms. He didn't like to call them "stretchers;" rather, fur forms. He did recommend shaping furs longer than wider for maximum appeal to fur buyers.

Bill admiring some of his well-handled fox furs. (Bill Nelson photo)

Bill advocated "clean skinning" beavers, and admitted he wasn't the fastest skinner there was. He stated there were a lot of trappers who had caught but a fraction of the beavers he had that could out-skin him by a long shot.

Years ago, Bill recommended the use of a hired skinner/fur handler for large-scale trapping. He said any wages paid to the helper would be well realized, in the long run.

Bill once wrote he was surprised at the fact that many trappers did not know fur quality and primeness nor how to grade their own furs. He encouraged them to visit fur buyers and fur houses and learn how to grade fur and view furs from different sections and compare them to furs from their area. He also recommended they read the few available books on furs and fur-grading to get a better understanding of the *"fur game."*

He even went as far to say that state laws should be enacted for trappers and hunters that required them to properly handle all furs they harvested, and if furs were wasted or deemed worthless from improper handling, this would result in a game violation. He also extended that to small and big game and fish. In other words, he didn't tolerate wasting furs and meat.

Bill had advice for dealing with fur buyers. *"Years ago, I used to do a lot of shipping to 2 or 3 of the leading fur houses. Later on, I began to sell furs to buyers that had special outlet for certain types of furs. Scout out these specialists and offer them nicely-handled pelts and you will receive top prices . . . It is a wise trapper that learns how to grade furs, correctly . . . Learn to grade and learn the actual market values as they really are; not what the grapevine and the big-league stove-warmers have to say. Grade out each type of fur into lots of #1s and good #2s, and then tally the sizes of large and extra large, medium, and small. Arrive at an average price-per-pelt. If the lots are far above average in size and quality, place a top, or bit above, top-market value on them. Decide right there how much each lot must bring and you are then ready to really do business with your buyers.*

Just keep in mind that the average buyer likes to see good furs brought in. Keep in mind, too, that they like to deal with a man that really knows what his furs are worth. If they know this, they will quickly quote you their top price."

Bill with some well-handled fox furs, ready for the fur buyer. (Photo courtesy of Ruth Peterson)

Bill suggested that trappers hold on to their furs until after season was over, if they could. He realized some could not, because they needed some operating money to continue trapping and said he had often been in that position. He recommended checking with several large country buyers fur buyers before shipping to a large, distant fur house. He also encouraged them to shop around and not get in the habit of selling to the same fur buyer, year after year. He got very angry with groups of country fur buyers who banded together with the same prices on furs, regardless of quality and quantity. "*It was enough to make a man think about the old six-gun law,*" he said. He complained that some fur buyers did not grade furs according to fur zones and did not really understand fur quality the way they should. He said they often threw all furs into one pile, regardless of the area they were taken from or primeness. He called this practice the "*rule-of-thumb*" grade. He warned fur buyers and houses not to take advantage of trappers with "*quick-buck*" deals and not to forget it was these trappers that were keeping them in business and to treat them with respect and fairness. He preferred the "*flat-price*" system of fur grading rather than high-grading select furs at a premium price and then "*scalping*" on the lower grades. He lamented the fact that many fur houses were only issuing one fur price list late in the season which did not accurately reflect what actual fur prices were. He noted that years ago, fur buyers were more competitive and issued several price lists throughout the season and quoted more current prices.

While trapping and traveling through various sections of the country, Bill made an effort to visit local or regional fur buyers and other trappers to examine fur specimens from those areas and to continue his never-ending quest to learn more about new species, fur types, and fur quality.

Sometime during the mid-1950s, Bill began to broker furs for other trappers. He only charged 5% commission, but the trapper had to pay all transportation and fur-house commission fees, etc. He told me this was a thankless job and after doing it for a few years, he was sorry he had begun doing it. He said that some of the trappers that sent him furs expected wonders and were very disappointed, or even mad, if they did not receive what they thought they should have. On the other hand, he said it was rewarding to hear gratitude from a lot of trappers he sold furs for, and to have them tell him they had received considerably more money by using him as a broker than what they could have obtained, locally. He was fussy about the furs he brokered, and would not accept "blue" early-caught furs or poorly-fleshed and handled furs. Not only was he concerned about the appearance of furs he sold for other trappers, his reputation to fur buyers and houses that he had dealt with for so many years, was on the line.

Chapter 17

THE INSTRUCTOR

Bill began selling personally-typed confidential trapping instructions in 1946. The prices ranged from $80 for mink, to $90 for fox, which later increased to $115. In 1947, he began to advertise personal in-the-field instructions at Farmington, IA during the months of April, May, and October. He charged $35 per day, or $50 for 2 days, for any species. Later, he quoted prices for instructions in his catalog as follows: fox and coyote "regular course" at $50 per day and an "extended course" with snow coverage and more coyote-wolf detail for $70; mink, $40; bobcat and cougar, $25; beaver and otter, $25; and 'coon, 'rat, skunk, etc., $25, and he would give instructions almost any month of the year, depending on his schedule.

In some of his ads, catalog, and book, he stated that he had instructed trappers in over half the states in the U.S. and portions of Canada. We have no way of knowing how many more he instructed from the time his catalog was printed, throughout the next decade, until his death.

Some of Bill's students went on to become noted trappers, lure makers, authors, and instructors, themselves. They included Ardell Grawe, Art Scott, George Good (deceased), and Craig O'Gorman. There may be more, but these are the ones I am aware of that publically-acknowledged taking instructions, either written or in the field, from him.

Besides Don Paul and Gus Gehlhar, I have heard about, or seen mentioned, several other student-partners of Bill's: Everett Swearingin, Ernal Olson, and Merle Meredith.

Chapter 18

THE AUTHOR

Judging from the articles I have gathered, Bill's writing career extended from 1935 through 1967. He was one of the most prolific trapping and outdoor authors of that time. His earlier articles in the 1930s were somewhat crude and lacked the unique style that he developed in the 1940s and which really blossomed during the 1950s, his most productive writing years. The few articles he wrote during the 1960s were classics, especially the 3-part series, "The Gray Ones." As I reviewed my collection of over 100 of his articles for this book, I was constantly reminded of all the things he had done and accomplished throughout his life. Thankfully, he was willing to share his knowledge and experiences with us over that 32-year period. One of the most impressive facts about Bill as an author was that he only had an 8th-grade education, but wrote as well as some college-educated authors. He also typed all his correspondence and manuscripts with an old manual typewriter that sat on the desk of his upstairs office. I can only speculate that he had a natural gift for writing and that his keen senses of observation and recall came into play while reading other writings and that he transferred some of that knowledge and style to his own. Both Harry Batten and Sonny Hootman suggested that Edith may have helped him with composition and editing since she had a high school education and had worked in an office for about 12 years before marrying Bill. One of the most classic examples of his unique writing style is the written descriptions he gave for trap-set locations in his predator trapping book. He used no photos or illustrations, yet you could clearly visualize in your mind the location he was describing and exactly where the trap should be set. Not long after his death and at the onsight of the fur boom of the 1970s and 1980s, other trapping books began to appear on the market, and some of them merely rehashed what he had already written over 15 years, before, and those authors used photos and/or illustrations to enhance the information. One only needs to read Bill's two trapping books and his articles to confirm this.

Bill even tried his hand at editing a magazine. He was listed as the editor for TRAPPER'S LIFE, a magazine published by George Bryant of Kentucky, in the January - February - March 1957 issue and for 3 more. Unfortunately, the magazine ceased publication after that last issue.

Since Bill died, I have read and heard other trappers and authors say that after reading some of his articles, they felt he hadn't told them anything, worthwhile, or that they didn't learn anything from reading them. Bill had an answer for them, 40 years ago. "*A few times down through the years, I have read and I have heard that I often write an article that leaves the trapper hanging in thin air. This, for the simple reason that I did not sit down and tell step-by-step how to construct a set that is already common knowledge to every farm-boy trapper in the nation. Personally, I see no reason for me to report that which has already been said and repeated in printed pages, thousands of times the past 50 years . . . I have done a little 'debunking' from time-to-time, and have tried to explain some of the 'little things' in this trapping game that are so very important. It will do no harm to mention here that I have received hundreds of letters from trappers that thanked me for passing along these little bits of fur-taking information . . . Anyway, seems that a lot of the boys feel the thin air I left them hanging in was healthy and held considerable merit.*" From a business standpoint, why would Bill go into detail on every aspect of what he was writing about for a one-shot payment of perhaps, $25-100 per article, when he was selling his books for $7 and $10, each, and giving personal instructions for $25-70 per day? Also, some of his articles were obviously written for the sheer pleasure and enjoyment of reading about his experiences. In other words, to entertain, not to instruct.

Following, is a list of the books, methods, and formulas that Bill authored during his career:

"Nelson's Superior Animal Lure Formulas", 1946
UNIT NUMBER ONE For The Fox and the Predator Trapper,
    4 pp

UNIT NUMBER TWO For The Water Trapper, 4 pp
UNIT NUMBER THREE For The Alpine and Northland Trapper, 4 pp

THE DIRT SET IN FREEZING WEATHER and COLD WEATHER TRICKS for the FOX AND COYOTE TRAPPER, 1947. 16 pp

Personal typewritten confidential instructions, 1946-1957
    Mink, 8 pp
    Fox, 8 pp
(These are the only two I have managed to collect)

The Nelson System For The Water Trapper, 1955. 48 pp

THE NELSON SYSTEM For The Coyote-Wolf-Bobcat-Fox and Cougar Trapper, 1957. 50 pp

THE NELSON SYSTEM FOR THE MARTEN AND ALPINE TRAPPER (Manuscript started, but never completed or book published) before he died. This may not have been the exact title he would have used, but I based it on the titles of his other two books)

"Nelson's SUPERIOR ANIMAL LURES" price list, mid- 1950s. 10 pp

CARE AND SALE OF FRESH-WATER PEARLS. 24 pp. Advertised in the Winter 1955 issue of THE WILDCRAFTERS WORLD AND SPORTSMAN'S TRADING POST magazine.

"NELSON'S SUPERIOR ANIMAL LURES" catalog, 1958 and/or 1963. 16 pp (Conflicting statements within the catalog suggested the catalog was printed on both dates and there was no definite date printed on the catalog)

From his catalog:
    NELSON'S DEEP-RIVER CATFISH FORMULA
    NELSON'S NO. 2 DEEP-RIVER CATFISH
        FORMULA
    NELSON'S CARP BAIT FORMULA
    NELSON'S TRAP & BASKET BAIT FORMULA
    HOW TO PROPERLY PREPARE CLAM BAITS

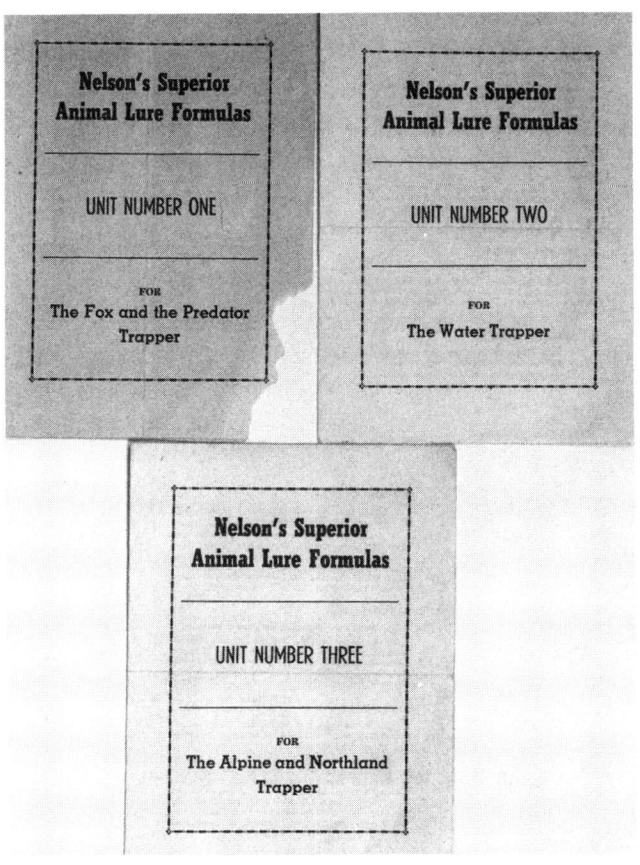

Bill's three units of lure formulas he released in 1946.
(Courtesy of Jack Harris)

THE DIRT SET IN FREEZING WEATHER

and

COLD WEATHER TRICKS

for the

FOX AND COYOTE TRAPPER

●

By
BILL NELSON

Bill's dirt antifreeze method booklet
he released in 1947.
(Courtesy of the late Rick Black)

Bill's water-trapping book he released in 1955.
(From the author's collection)

Bill's predator-trapping book he released in 1957.
(From the author's collection)

One of Bill's personal magazines to which he furnished
the front-cover photograph of a scene along his
marten trapline in the Sierras.
(From the author's collection)

Another of Bill's personal magazines to which he furnished the front-cover photo of a scene along his marten trapline in the Sierras.
(From the author's collection)

Another front-cover photo of Bill and a
marten catch in the Sierras.
(From the author's collection)

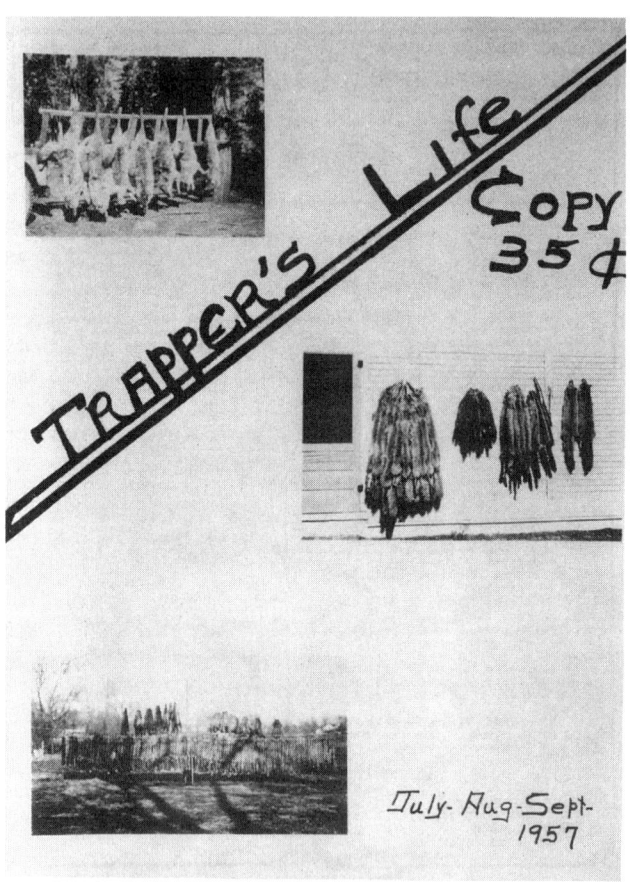

Front cover of TRAPPER'S LIFE magazine
designed by Bill with his photos, while he was editor.
(From the author's collection)

Another front cover of TRAPPER'S LIFE magazine designed by Bill with his photos, while he was editor. (From the author's collection)

The following list is the magazine articles I have in my collection:

HUNTER-TRADER-TRAPPER:
1935-Nov "Reeds Lake Bass", p 19
1936-Jun "Famous Guides Opinions . . . Bill Nelson", pp 3-4
         "Pike And Muskies", pp 9-10, 33
   -Sep "Tiger Muskies", pp 9-10, 24
1937-Nov "Few And Far Between", pp 17-18

HUNTER-TRADER-TRAPPER OUTDOORSMAN:
1938-Nov "Late Fall Muskies", pp 15, 40

NORTH AMERICAN TRAPPER:
1936-1(2) "Trapper", pp 10-11

THE TRAPPER:
1937-Dec "Cat-Footed Grays", pp 11, 13-14

THE TRAPPER & SPORTSMAN:
1938-Jan "Trapping Ridge Reds", pp 3, 14-15

WESTERN TRAPPER:
1935-Oct Bill's photo on front cover
         "Traplines Of The North", pp 3-7, 11
1939-Dec "A Few Photos Sent In By Bill Nelson", p 4
1941-Nov "The Visible And Other Sets", pp 3-6, 16, 18

OUTDOORSMAN:
1942-Jan "Speaking Of Cats", pp 12-14, 34-36

OUTDOORSMAN HUNTER-TRADER-TRAPPER:
1943-Nov/Dec "Bobcat Facts And Fancies", pp 16-17, 43, 45

THE WILDCRAFTERS WORLD:
1947-Mar "Six Sable Chokers", pp 14-15
    -Dec "Freshwater Pearls-Care And Sale Of, Pt I",
         pp 13-19

THE TRAPPERS WORLD:
1947-Jul "Once Upon A Time There Was A Fox", pp 5-7
   -Aug "So You Want To Trap Marten, Pt I", pp 5-7
   -Sep "So You Want To Trap Marten, Pt II", pp 5-6, 26

1948-Feb "Gray Ramblers Of The Hills, Pt I", pp 5-7, 32
   -May "Gray Ramblers Of The Hills, Pt II", pp 5, 12-14
   -Jul/Aug Bill's photos on front cover
           "Mink On The Stretchers, Preface- Tricks Of
             The Game", pp 4-6, 22
1949-Jan Illustration by Philip Newberg sent in by Bill Nelson
          on front cover
           "Mink On The Stretchers- Baits And Lures,
             Chapter 2", pp 6-7
   -Feb/Mar Bill's photo on front cover
           "Mink On The Stretchers- Baits And Lures",
             pp 5-7, 15

FINS-SKINS-GAME:
1950-Aug "The Painted Trout Of Gold Valley", pp 4-8
   -Oct   "Bones", pp 59-66

AMERICAN WOODSMAN:
1951-Jul "Trail Of The Sable", pp 10-13, 31

TRAPPER SPORTSMAN:
1950-Jul/Aug "Bobcat Prospect, Pt I", pp 3-4, 16
   -Sep   "Bobcat Prospect, Pt II", pp 9-11, 24
   -Nov/Dec "Simple Fur Taking For Beginner And
               Professional", pp 4-6, 22
1951-Jan/Feb "Bobcat Trickery", pp 4-6, 24
   -Sep   "Land Trappers", pp 6-7
   -Nov/Dec "Sierra Journey, Pt I", pp 4-7
1952-Jan/Feb "Sierra Journey, Pt II", pp 7-11, 26
   -Jul/Aug "Music On The River", pp 2-9
   -Nov/Dec "Wolf Wolf", pp 4-6
1953-Jul/Aug "Notes On Fur Taking", pp 2-7
1954-Sep/Oct "I'll Take Musky", pp 2-6
1955-Jan/Feb "Rendezvous With Sable", pp 2-6

TRAPPER'S LIFE:
1954-Oct   "The Mink Line", 4 pp unnumbered
1955-Jul   "Fur Sign & Trap Lore", pp 5-13, 15-17, 22-23
1956-Apr/May/Jun "Winter Traplines, Pt I", pp 7-8, 11
    -Jul/Aug/Sep "Winter Traplines, Pt II", pp 8, 18-19
    -Oct/Nov/Dec "Woodland Trails, Pt I", pp 17-20
1957-Jan/Feb/Mar "Woodland Trails, Pt II", pp 7-8
    -Apr/May/Jun "Woodland Trails, Pt III", pp 6, 10-17
    -Jul/Aug/Sep Bill's photos on front cover
                  "Market Notes For Wildcrafters", pp 7, 16
    -Oct/Nov/Dec Bill's photos on front cover
                  "Fur-Fun & Profit, Pt I", pp 9-10, 20
                  "From The Hills And Waterways",
                   pp 11-12
                  "Pearl Market Facts", pp 15-16

THE NATIONAL TRAPPER'S DIGEST:
1956-Apr/May/Jun "Adventures With Sable", pp 4-13
1957-Jan/Feb/Mar "Montana Prospect, Pt I", pp 4-9
   -Spring   "Montana Prospect, Pt II", pp 16-21, 29
   -Summer   "Fur Fact & Fiction, Pt I", pp 10-17
1958-Oct   "Fur Fact & Fiction, Pt II", pp 8-15
1959-May/Jun   "Fur Fact & Fiction, Pt III", pp 4-7

FUR-FISH-GAME:
1935-Sep   "The Fish Bug Bites", pp 22-25
            "Coon & Trapping Methods", p 44
    -Oct   "Prospecting The Line", pp 48-51
1936-Mar   "Woodland Gold", pp 42-43
    -Jun   "The Lynx Cat", pp 50-52
    -Aug   "Looking Back", pp 50-51
    -Nov   "Professional Wildcrafting, Pt I", pp 13-16
            "Hidden Pockets", pp 34-35, 41
    -Dec   "Professional Wildcrafting, Pt II", pp 16-19
1937-Jan   "Wolf Wolf", pp 8-9, 15
            "Iowa Trappers", p 53
    -May   "Northward Bound", pp 10-12
            "Ginseng In Iowa", pp 46-47

	-Nov	"Trapping The Farmland Reds", pp 10-12, 16
	-Dec	"Back To Iowa", pp 12-13
1938	-Feb	"Medical Roots For Profit", pp 44-45, 55
	-Mar	"North Trails", pp 8-9, 55
	-Apr	"Trapping The Furbearers", pp 14-16
	-May	"Fishing The Big Rivers", pp 15-18
	-Jul	"Pearl Hunting For Profit", pp 12-14, 17-18
	-Dec	Photo of Bill, p 44
1941	-Mar	2 photos by Bill, p 21
	-Jul	"You Never Get Over It", pp 46-47
1942	-Sep	"The Nomad Trapper, Pt I", pp 15-18, 39
	-Oct	"The Nomad Trapper, Pt II", pp 17-18
	-Dec	"Condemned But Why", pp 13-16
		"On The Trails For 'Seng", pp 34-35
1946	-Jun	"Alpine Trapline, Pt I", pp 48-52
	-Jul	"Alpine Trapline, Pt II", pp 36-39
	-Aug	"The Golden Sable Of Mystery Basin", pp 14-15, 40
	-Nov	"Bobcat Chatter", pp 12-13, 15
	-Dec	"Middle Fork Journey", pp 11-12, 29
1947	-Jan	"Men On Long Skis", pp 13-14, 20
		Photo of Bill, p 46
	-Jun	"Fresh Water Gems", pp 10-11, 32-35
	-Aug	"Harvest In The Woodlands", pp 44-45
1948	-Jan	"Marten Facts & Fancies", pp 48, 50-53
1949	-Aug	"Foxing The Fox", pp 10-11, 38-39
1950	-Feb	"Down Trappers Trails", pp 10-11, 50-53
	-Mar	"Marten Trapping Facts", pp 12-13, 49-50
1951	-Jan	"An Art In Itself", pp 12-13, 42-43
	-Jun	"Meet The Gray Ghost", pp 12-13, 39-40
	-Sep	"Land Or Water", pp 10-11, 40-41
	-Nov	"Coyote Damn Foolery", pp 46-50
1952	-Feb	"Idle Thoughts From The Outdoors", pp 12-13, 42-43
	-Jun	"Thunder In The North", pp 13-14, 52-53
1953	-Feb	"Trapping Facts-Condensed", pp 11-12, 52-54
	-May	"Lets Look At Pearls", pp 14, 22-24
	-Aug	"Fur Facts And Theories", pp 10-11, 46-48

-Dec	"Bobcat Fiddle Dee-Dee", pp 14-15, 48-49
1954-May	"Catfishing Is Fun", pp 20-26
1957-Feb	"Around The States With Fox & Coyote", pp 44-54
-Sep	"Rimrock Outlaws", pp 42-47
-Nov	"Steel Trap Trail, Pt I", pp 16-17, 46-48
	"A Few Fighting Words", pp 53-54
-Dec	"Steel Trap Trail, Pt II", pp 18-19, 51-52
	"Tips, Trap Talk, & Techniques", pp 40-47
1958-Jan	"Steel Trap Trail, Pt III", pp 46-48
-Nov	"Fur Trail Talk", pp 9-11, 42-48
-Dec	"Winter Fur Trail", pp 9-11, 42-48
1959-Jan	"A Few More Mink", pp 10-11, 38-42
-Dec	"My 1958 Trapline, Pt I", pp 16-17, 48-52
1960-Jan	"My 1958 Trapline, Pt II", pp 46-49
1962-Nov	"The Gray Ones, Pt I", pp 18-19, 52-55
-Dec	"The Gray Ones, Pt II", pp 45-50
1963-Jan	"The Gray Ones, Pt III", pp 44-48
-Dec	"From Fur Shed To Market", pp 16-17, 42-50
1967-Jun	"Summer Golden Harvest", pp 50-51

There are probably more articles he wrote, but these are the ones I have managed to collect for the past 31 years. Two articles he mentioned in one of his articles are listed below and I was never able to locate them.

Magazine, Year, Month- Unknown,   "Camp Plenty"
                                  "More About 'Cats"

Chapter 19

SAYINGS, PHRASES, AND BULLET WORDS

Bill used some catchy, and sometimes humorous, words, phrases, sayings, and expressions when he was talking, in his letters, in his articles, and in his ads. One time when I was at their place, Edith was going on and on about something (I don't remember what it was) and Bill finally said to her, "*Get down to earth, woman,*" then looked at me, and winked and grinned. Below are listed some of these items that were provided to me by several of his colleagues, and others, I extracted from his writings, ads, etc. I am not saying he originated all of them, but he used them throughout his life, both verbally and in print.

"All things being equal, he who works the hardest, goes the farthest"
"If you want something bad enough, you must pay the price, and the price is not always the money"
"Peckernecks" were trap thieves and other undesirables
"High-balling"
"Long-Lining"
"Heap" as in "Heap good fur catch"
"Superior Animal Lures"
"Enviable reputation"
"Without a near parallel"
"Deadliest"
"Copy-the-Nelson-way"
"Dope" referring to lure
"Strict Departure"
"Cut rate"
"Cranks"
"Splashy"
"Big-spread advertising"
"Dingo"
"You listen here, Murphy"
"Uppercrust do-gooders"
"Chap"
"Poppycock"

"Blood and thunder"
"Pseudo-experts"
"Wouldn't even make a good watch fob"
"Country scalpers" were fur buyers who took advantage of trappers
"Green-eyed boys/lads"
"Bar none"
"Vastly unlike"
"Dollar-a-bottle argument"
"Slobber and dig"
"Penetrating, fragrant"
"Wonder lure"
"Departure from"
"Put up your money, chalk, or marbles"
"Mouth-slobbering interest"
"We are not dead, yet"
"Loaded"
"Debunk the bunk"

As serious as he was, it was good Bill had a "light" side, too.

Chapter 20

THE NATURALIST AND STUDENT

Bill considered himself to be a naturalist and a student of wildlife and the outdoors, in general. He read a lot and had the ability to retain the facts and knowledge from what he read. Several articles he wrote over the years pertained to the species and subspecies of several furbearers and predators. He described them, one by one, by name and the geographical area they were located in, descriptions of fur quality, habits, etc. *"I have always been very much interested in species classification and especially in the many races of wolves, bobcats, and coyotes and I have spent a lot of time making a study of such animals. It is a fascinating study and I am always much interested in any and all stories that have to do with them. I am interested in any casual observations and I am most interested in carefully-compiled 'fact-findings'."* He mentioned reading works by famous naturalists of that time: Joseph Grinnell, Joseph Dixon, and Jean Lindsdale. He undoubtedly read the classics by J. Frank Dobie, Stanley P. Young and Goldman, etc.

Bill stated there were 3 species and one subspecies of bobcats shown in this photo of part of his 1941-42 catch in CA. (Bill Nelson photo)

In fact, one of Bill's articles on bobcats was even used as a reference in Stanley P. Young's classic book, THE BOBCAT OF NORTH AMERICA, which remains the standard reference for bobcat biology and classification, to this day. I am not aware of any other trapping authors of that era whose works were cited in a major reference book.

As mentioned, Bill started taking notes on observations he made in the field, trapline events, catches, sex and weights of trapped animals, etc. at any early age and continued these documentations throughout his career. Therefore, he had facts to recall, not speculations or efforts to recall from memory.

When he was a kid, Bill mentioned catching hybrid catfish that appeared to be a cross between blues and channels. He also saw this hybridism in northern MN with muskies and northern pike which are called tiger muskies.

Bill noted he heard his first cougar vocalizations in the Trinity Mountains of CA while trapping with Jack Foster during the season of 1939-40. It was within a hundred yards of him when he first heard it. He said it did not scream, but rather gave out strange growls, snarls, and caterwauls for 5 minutes before it finally moved out of hearing range.

While trapping wolves in northern MN during the 1930s, he thought the most common subspecies he was trapping was Canis lupus lyacon, but he also trapped some larger specimens he speculated might have been crossed with Canis lupus nubilus, a larger subspecies found west of MN. He also reported some very large wolves be taken in isolated areas in MN that he guessed might be Canis lupus occidentalis. During this time, he also observed and wrote about an unusual interaction between a wolf and a pack of coyotes. He came across a deer that had been apparently killed by a pack of coyotes. Upon closer examination, he discovered the tracks of a huge lone wolf amongst the coyote tracks. The year before, he had heard a lone wolf howl in this same area, and it was quickly answered by several coyotes. He wondered if this lone wolf actually traveled with the pack of coyotes and that it may have been their leader, or if the pack of coyotes just followed him around, feeding on his kills, after he was done with them.

One of Bill's most famous observations he wrote about in several of his articles and in his books was how populations of fox, coyote, marten, mink, etc. will *"drift"* or migrate to and from areas within a short period of time. He cited several examples of how his catches would fluctuate directly with these drifts and he advised trappers who experienced a drop-off in their catches after trapping an area for a period of time to hang in there, since the animals would probably drift back in, later.

He observed how, sometimes, foxes would move out of an area when coyotes entered it, but they would move back in after the coyotes left. He also wrote of the *"fall shuffle"* or dispersal of pups during the fall months.

During the early 1950s, Bill predicted coyotes would invade his area of southeastern IA where they were hardly present, then. He attributed this to land-use changes due to farms being vacated and croplands being turned back into pastures and brush fields which created better coyote habitat. His prediction came true during the mid-to-late 1960s. The fact that he wanted to run a full-time trapline for coyotes in 1970, as discussed in the Introduction, is evidence he thought coyote populations were adequate for such an effort. He told me the most coyotes he had trapped in a season there in southeast IA, up to that time, was 17, and these were trapped incidental to running traplines for fox.

Regarding hybrids and coydogs, Bill noticed they seemed to occur more in areas where coyotes were previously absent, more so than in traditional coyote-inhabited areas. He speculated it might be due to the ability of coyotes to adapt to more-populated areas of humans and domestic dogs and their ability to reproduce readily, even with other canids. He noted that a coyote having as little as 1/8 blood-line from a larger dog such as a collie, shepherd, or German police would produce a large offspring. He also mentioned the cross-breeding of red wolves with coyotes, dogs, and coydogs and what a nightmare it would be for subspecie classification.

Bill predicted the invasion of coyotes to southeastern IA. Here he is with the proof, years later. (Bill Nelson photo)

Bill predicted the return of red wolves to IA, too. He said they were present in small numbers when he was a kid and they still existed in small numbers in areas of MO and AR. He described the characteristics of a red wolf. "*A coarser and bristly fur, developed manes, heavier feet, highly-developed canine teeth, heavily-cusped premolar teeth, black tail and leg markings, and a heavier and longer skull than coyotes.*" His prediction came true as he stated in a letter to Bill Waterman on March 10, 1969 that he had already trapped 17 of them by that time and they weighed from 50-109 pounds. Remember, too, the red wolf pelt I already described that was hanging on his living room wall. He told Gus Gehlhar he had trapped some of those red wolves in MO, though, not far from the IA border.

Bill was well known and respected for his knowledge of canids. Ron McIntosh said of him, "Bill was truly an expert on the canines. When the IA Conservation Commission wanted to know something about canines, they came to Bill."

From years of experience, Bill noted that foxes, coyotes, and wolves ran in groups far more than many people realized. "*Do not ask me why, because I do not know. But, I have long observed this habit and I have made good use of it.*"

Bill made an extensive study of marten species classification and even corresponded with naturalists in Russia and other far away countries to learn more about the Russian sable, Baum, stone, and Japanese martens. He wrote several articles describing his findings. He was very interested in Martes caurina humboldtensis, or the Humboldt or California coastal marten. He first trapped them during the 1938-39 season and again during the 1941-42 season. He said their life zones varied from a few hundred feet above sea level to over 2,000'. He remembered trapping one closer to 3,000'. He described them as being smaller than those found in the Trinities and Cascades, as well as those he trapped in the Sierras. He said their fur was shorter, but denser and more dark-colored. "*Cocoa to mummy brown,*" as he put it. All the specimens he trapped were dark; no pales. He noted they had an extremely bright-orange throat patch and also a long ventral orange patch. Their feet lacked the usual "*snowshoe-pad*" construction of their high-country cousins. They were also more lanky and longlegged. The CA Fish and Game thought these Humboldt marten were extinct until Bill showed them the specimens he had trapped and generously shared with them all the written data and notes he had collected. He recommended the season be closed on them for their protection. After 4 years of prodding by him, full protection was given to the Humboldt marten.

Chapter 21

THE LURE MAKER

"There is no black magic to lure making. A really good lure is simply something that is developed by an experienced man through hard work, extensive field study, endless experiments, and the spending of a lot of cold cash. Working and developing a good lure takes patience and exacting work, much the same as the making of a costly perfume. There are a lot of tricks to blending the right amount of the right ingredient. It is not a game of tossing a lot of glands and musks together in a haphazard manner, as so many may think, nor are good lures the result of an accident."

Bill's reputation as an animal lure maker was a close second, if not equal to, his reputation as a trapper. He started making his own lures back in 1920, at the age of 12. *"My first bottle of self-made animal scent broke in my school desk and ran down the leg to the floor. It smelled pretty rotten, and I had a mess to clean up and I stayed after school for a good many evenings, because of it . . . True rhodium oil could still be had and worked quite well with native musks and oils for mink. The lures I used on skunk and 'possum were mixtures of rotted muskrat musk, catfish oil, anise oil, asafetida, and skunk musk. Brother, when a bottle of that material happened to pop a cork at school, things really happened . . . I bought a lot of lures and threw most of them in the river. I made up dozens and dozens of mixtures of my own; others were from the usual 1,001 "floater" formulas being sold at that time. I used catnip, honey, anise, and angelica. I mixed calamus and muskrat musk and many fruit flavors and pure extracts purchased from an old-time German druggist. Some of my sets smelled like a fruit stand on a sunny street; others smelled like a wrecked drug store. I will not mention how some of my sets up in the hills smelled. One old trapper trapping along the same stream I was, said he could smell my sets a mile off. I was interested in that since I was taking as much fur as he was."*

Bill learned that carcasses of animals he trapped made good baits. *"I finally learned to save all my skunk carcasses and to use them to very good advantage. This brought one heap of civet cats, skunks, and 'possums to bag. It also meant the taking of some foxes along the large sand bars and even added no few 'coon pelts to the fur shed collection."* Later, he developed a bait that was so stinky and powerful, *"I could hardly stand it, myself."* After catching a few feral housecats in some of his sets, he observed how attractive they were to fox and coyote and later when he trapped in northern MN, to wolves and even bobcats. He used the whole cat carcass at sets, along with lure and urine. A few years later, he developed his famous *"cut bait"* using chunks of housecat meat soaked in a bait solution he developed. He also tried baits made from woodchuck, skunk, and beaver, but stated that housecat was the *"king flesh"* for his bait. After he placed his bait on the market and the demand grew, he was forced to use chunks of beaver meat for most of the bait he sold, since it was more readily available in quantity. Sonny Hootman told me he would drive his pickup to Creston, IA to pick up a whole truck load of beaver carcasses for Bill from Henry Hainline, a fur farmer and fur buyer. Henry also collected urines from his caged animals and Bill bought urines from him, wholesale, to use on his traplines and he also repackaged and sold urines in retail quantities. Bill told Gus Gehlhar when meat bait became hard to get, he would even use chunks of fish, and they worked well. Bill used chunks of meat for baits, he didn't grind the meat into a paste. He began selling his bait in 1947 for $1.75 per pint. When he started prebaiting his sets before season, he observed that fox and coyote would seldom eat the baits. They would dig them out, roll on them, sometimes urinate on them, a few would carry them off a short distance, and a very few would cache them. He was proud of the fact few foxes or coyotes would pass his bait up without responding to it, and since they didn't eat it, he concluded his bait worked whether the animal was hungry, or not.

Bill continued to experiment with and develop new lures into his early adulthood. *". . . All this time, I was working with scents, creating new ones and improving old ones; in some cases, discarding old ones. This took a lot of time and a lot of work. It also meant the spending of a lot of dollars and I invested a bit over*

$1,000 during those early years for my scent experiments." He tested single ingredients and blends of ingredients. "Such individual odors of skunk essence, rotted fish or blood odor, carrion odor, and single animal musks of any kind are of very limited value. I may also say that NO musk or urine from any animal will make another animal run around in a swimming red rage. Any and all of the above odors do have value when properly blended with other valuable odors, properly aged and fixed, and placed in a good vehicle . . . It has taken me as long as 10 years to perfect a lure to the point where I would pronounce it, good . . . Many scent sellers speak mysteriously about rare imported musks, while others strictly maintain that a line of local musks and essential oils are as good or better than the imported ones. I agree with neither schools of thought. I have learned that many of my pet formulas would be worthless without the imported musks and equally as worthless without our native musks and certain essential oils. They all have a place and a value." Regarding the theory that certain musks and urines caused rage in some animals, he wrote there was a fad for using mink musk an "enrager" for trapping otters. He called this "bunk" and said he knew of 6 odors that were far more attractive to otters than mink musk, but of course he didn't identify them, since he probably used them in his otter lures. He had the same thing to say about using weasel musk in mink lures and stated there were at least 20 odors more attractive to mink than that.

 Several of Bill's associates told me he had received formal training in ingredients and formulations through a perfumery course he took which cost $350, but none of them knew exactly when this occurred or if it was a home-study course or actual resident training. That was a lot of money in those days and it emphasized his commitment to learning more about the business and producing better lures. I am not aware of any other lure maker at that time, or since, that had that kind of formal training and it was to his advantage. As he mentioned, an old German druggist also helped him with formulations and obtaining lure ingredients. In those days, most drug stores sold, or could obtain, many of the ingredients that were used in making animal and fish lures such as anise oil, rhodium oil, valerian extract, Tonquin musk grains, catnip and other essential oils, etc. and most pharmacists had a basic knowledge of compounding and blending those ingredients.

After trapping bobcats in MN and CA and testing lures on them, he wrote, "*Many years ago, I learned the fact that bobcats are far from being cold nosed. All cats, including a pet tabby, have a very keen and highly-developed sense of smell. Make some tests on a common housecat, some day, and you will begin to see the light on that moth-eaten fallacy about cold-nosed cats . . . I have spent more money on developing really deadly bobcat lures than I have on any other types of lure. Marten and mink were close runner-ups.*"

Bill spent many years on his traplines in several states and under all weather conditions, developing and testing lures for all the animals he trapped. It was not until 1946 that he decided to offer his lure formulas for sale to the public. A magazine ad appeared in August 1946 and in the literature for them he stated, "*At this time, I am too busy trapping and following my wildcrafting to bother with a scent-selling business. Therefore, I am placing my formulas on the market, instead.*" Also in the literature he sent out describing these formulas, he wrote, "*During my many years on the traplines, I have used and discarded hundreds of the old formulas that have been handed down and passed around since the dawn of trapping. And I have used a lot of prepared scents: good, bad, and indifferent. The past 20 years I have perfected and used only the formulas that I describe in the units I have for sale. They are my own, and they take fur. My formulas are not what you could term as 'stink baits.' I discarded any and all so-called stink baits and lures, many years ago. A chunk of rotten horse meat is as good as the best of them, and a ripe skunk carcass, a darn sight better. Nor are my dopes made up of a cup of fish oil, a dash of anise, a fist-full of castor, and a squirt of skunk musk. Good luring is simply not done that way.*" He sold the formulas as "Superior Animal Lure Formulas" and offered them in 3 units. Unit Number One covering fox, coyote, and bobcat for $7, Unit Number Two covering mink, otter, 'coon, muskrat, and beaver for $5.50, and Unit Number Three covering marten, fisher, and weasel for $3.50. He offered all 3 units for $10.

For reasons he never explained or wrote about, Bill began to advertise and sell his lures, a few months after he released the formulas for sale. Some of the lures he sold had the same names as the ones in the formulas. At that time, he changed the name of the formulas to just "Nelson's Lure Formulas," since the lures he sold were named, "Nelson's Superior Animal Lures," the name they carried until his death. Years later in his catalog, he described the 3 units of lure formulas he still sold, *"These are old and time-proven formulas that were used by Nelson for many years along his traplines. They are not to be confused with the dollar-specials that flood the market. These formulas result in lures that are second only to the Nelson's Superior Lures in the form that they are offered in, today, and which are made from closely-guarded formulas that are priceless."* He obviously had improved and perfected the lures he originally sold the formulas for, as well as developing new lures whose formulas weren't previously sold. He increased the prices of the formulas in the catalog to $10, $7, and $5, respectively, or $20 for all 3 units.

Bill offered two main types of lures: call lures and gland lures. His call lures were not the same as what the call lures of today are, namely skunk and/or other strong odors. He described his call lures in an old price list, *"No Nelson lure is a haphazard mixture of cheap oils, castor, and bargain-counter musks. They are not skunk essence nose-burners, nor are they cheap and dollar-hunting mixtures of fish oils and carrion odors. They are unique and expertly-blended odors that contain the world's most costly, rare, and unusual luring essentials . . . A good call lure is the trapper's most valuable bit of trapline equipment. A good call lure is many, many times more attractive than any gland lure mixture known to man, and that includes my own . . . Good call lures will more than double your take of furs and scalps . . . Call lures are very long-lasting and will withstand weather conditions that render gland lures, worthless . . . A Nelson call-type lure will improve with age up to 10 years . . . the bottle will, of course, have to be well-sealed and stored away from direct light."* Anyone who used Bill's lures will remember they were exactly as he described them. They were not rotten smelling or dominated by skunk odor. Rather, they were what I would term as, "powerfully fragrant," and no one odor dominated the lures although each lure had its own unique odor. He definitely knew how to fix and preserve lures, too. I have several bottles of his original lures in my collection that are 30-40 years old and are still potent and smell the same as they did, then. He described his gland lures, "NOT thin mixtures of a few glands, some urine, and a bit of base. Neither have any one been rendered next to worthless through the addition of undesirable oils, chemicals, or carrion odors, of any type. Each one is made, blended, fixed, and based in a manner that will supply the absolute maximum 'animal odor' . . . a Nelson gland lure will improve up to 5-6 years."

Bill had 22 call lures and 10 gland-type lures for almost all furbearers and predators for sale as well as his famous fox and coyote bait, the bait solution, itself, a deer lure, a fish lure oil, two catfish baits, and a carp oil. While most lures of that era sold for $1.00 per ounce bottle, Bill priced his lures at $1.00-2.50 per bottle. He said, "I cannot make a lure and sell it for a dollar after investing more than that in the lure, itself." A few years after his catalog was issued, he wrote on the front covers of catalogs he sent out from then on, "All prices advanced 10%" to compensate for increased production and mailing costs. He did not print a new catalog, however.

Besides his lures, bait, etc., Bill also sold some lure ingredients which he said were "over and above my own needs and as a convenience to the trapper," as well as trap wax and resin. He was proud of his lures and said they were used in all of the states, much of Canada, and in some foreign countries. He stated his business was based on repeat business and word-of-mouth advertising by his current customers to other trappers. He said, "My primary goal is producing lures that will give the trapper the greatest possible return in fur and bounty dollars" and he "Used ingredients not commonly used, if at all, by other lure makers." He claimed he had boxes full of testimonial letters, from many, of his customers that he would gladly show to anybody, anytime. He stated, "I do not make claims that I am not willing and very able to prove." Harry Batten said of Bill's lures, "Bill made the best lures there ever were." Sonny Hootman said, "Bill built his lures; and his business out of quality. His heart was in them. He beat them all at lure making." Ron

NELSON'S
SUPERIOR ANIMAL LURES

THE NELSON LURES
ARE INTERNATIONALLY FAMOUS

They have earned an enviable reputation that is without a near parallel. Wherever the fur trapper and the predator control man operates, you will find Nelson Lures.

BILL NELSON
FARMINGTON, IOWA

This was Bill's only catalog he issued in 1958 and/or 1963, although he had price lists before it was printed. (From the author's collection)

McIntosh said, "I think his work with lures is perhaps unqualed. He had some complex formulas and every bottle smelled the same as the last." Ron said he caught 127 muskrats on a one-ounce bottle of Bill's lure. From my years of using them, I couldn't add anything that wasn't already said, above.

Bill was understandably very secretive about the exact ingredients and composition of his lures and bait, other than the ingredients listed in his catalog. His student partners were directed to collect glands and parts from the carcasses of animals they skinned which were placed in clean glass jars and Bill took it from there. Don Paul said Bill had jars of glands, meat bases, etc. in various stages of aging and decomposition, buried all over his yard. He also said Bill would trap mice in the yard and he had his neighbors trap them, too, which he used in some of his lures. Sonny Hootman used to sun-render and collect catfish juice for Bill and I already mentioned that Bill would save some clam meats for use in lures, too. Although Sonny was a neighbor to Bill for several years and accompanied him hunting, fishing, and trapping, he said Bill never told him anything about lure and bait making.

After Bill died, Jack Harris obtained the names of two ingredient suppliers that Bill had used, from Edith. They were Beacon Chemical Company in NY and Neuman-Buslee-Wolfe in IL. Both companies have long been sold and absorbed into large fragrance company conglomerates.

Bill had shelves of his lures, all bottled and labeled, in his attic. They were neatly arranged, according to type and quantity. He was the only luremaker I knew of that sealed bottles of lure with wax. He melted wax in a can and dipped the caps and necks of each bottle into the melted wax, which formed an air-tight seal. He sometimes used amber-glass bottles for his lures, which helped keep out certain light rays which could deteriorate some of the lure ingredients before the lures were used. When you received bottles of Bill's lures in the mail, they were well-packed in newspaper and no odors were emitted from the box they came in. This was just another one of his unique ways of doing business. Marlene Rider told me that Bill kept a lot of his lure materials in Forrest Rider's barn and actually made the lures, there.

Jack Harris was a dealer for Bill's lures for around 13 years. Both he and Ron McIntosh, another dealer, said Bill would give them a 35% discount on lures, but there was a $100 minimum order, to start with. Jack said Bill preferred his dealers order at least $100 worth of lures on subsequent orders, too, but did ship orders for amounts less than that. At the time Bill's catalog was printed, he stated he had 5 dealers, but in a letter to Bill Waterman dated March 18, 1969, he wrote he had 11, then.

As good as Bill's lures were, he even admitted that some animals would get smart to them if they were used in the same area too long and he recommended trappers use other types/brands of lures for a season or two. He told several people to use Herb Lenon's lures, then, as he thought they were second only to his.

Regarding how much of his lures to use at a set, Bill wrote, "*Personally, I have never made use of eye droppers, counting out drops of lure, nor feather or twig applicators. I use lure by generous applications that might be called 'gobs'. Let me assure you that an animal must smell what you offer before it can want, what you offer.*" Don Paul and Gus Gehlhar both told me that Bill used a gob of thicker lure about the size of a lima bean and with liquid lures, he just poured out a "good amount," without counting drops. He used about an ounce of urine at new sets and about half that at remake sets.

Bill died before he could instruct a successor how to make those great lures. Don Paul said that Bill told him there were a lot of things about his lures he just kept in his head and didn't write them down, so he took that knowledge to the grave. I'm sure he's "Up There" looking down with a gleam in those dark eyes and a smirk on his face saying, "*Keep try'in, boys.*"

Chapter 22

THE MAN

"Life is to be experienced, not contemplated."

I'll begin this chapter by quoting some comments and stories by some of Bill's best friends and associates.

Harry Batten: "Bill Nelson was a common guy. He thought the land owed him a living . . . He was a loner . . . He was very motivated and wouldn't give up on anything . . . He was very particular and fussy."

Sonny Hootman: "He lived his whole life just as he chose. He was no doubt the best there ever was in his own field and all around in the outdoors . . . He was an excellent writer, maybe even a little too sharp . . . He was a great guy, a good friend in his own way, and I learned a lot from him: how to trap, about the woods, and how not to be deceived and taken in by, smooth BS . . . He never had much money. He was just happy being Bill Nelson. Had he lived just a very few more years, he would have been what would have been rich, to Bill . . . He enriched the lives of others while he was here. This is the real success few men ever achieve."

Don Paul: "Bill was a teacher, protector, companion, and friend, all in one package . . . Easy to like, admire, and want to emulate . . . The most remarkable person I have ever known . . . Tough, but kind . . . Fierce competitor, but respectful of the other person . . . He did not generally put people down. . . If he liked you, you had a wonderful friend. If he didn't, it would be best to leave him alone . . . He could very well have been at home with the early settlers, traders, trappers, etc. that opened up the frontier in the early 1800s . . . In my mind, he was always likened to a native American Indian in his ways, thoughts, and treatment of animals . . . An outdoorsman is so independent! They march to a different drummer. No one else understands that . . . He was not a bragger . . . Anything he was connected to for very long had to be durable, quick, and steady. He did not take well to mediocrity. Looking back, it seems impossible that one man could be so expert in so many areas. It seemed everything he tackled, he excelled in . . . He was a good listener, good teacher, and best of all, a loyal friend to the deserving. Add to this his incredible stamina, will to excel, and the mental toughness to push his body to incredible limits. At this time, I cannot think of any two men, put together, that could equal his abilities. Surprisingly, in all of this, was his humbleness. Lucky was the person who was able to know and call him, 'friend' . . . He was a very hard worker . . . He worked intelligently . . . He was honest . . . He had tremendous physical abilities . . . He was organized to the extreme . . . He led a satisfying life, but was always just one serious injury from disaster . . . He enjoyed life . . . He was a true conservationist . . . He was very partial to animals. He was kind to them. He wanted them to have no suffering. He would be rough with a person who did not dispatch them quickly and humanely. He said they suffered enough in their life without us adding to it. He wanted them to experience less suffering than anything nature may have had in store for them . . . I never ceased to miss him after he died and the void seems greater as time goes by. It is especially painful to me that I never made more effort to get back and see him in person, more often."

Jack Harris: "Bill was strongly opinionated and believed in what he said. He was very competitive." Jack related a story where his sons and Bill were target-shooting with a dart pistol and one of his sons continually beat Bill in the competition. Jack said he could tell this really bothered Bill.

John Barbee first met Bill while he lived at Fort Madison, IA and was trapping mink in that area. While checking some sets around a railroad bridge, a guy hollered at him from the top of the bridge and informed John that he was trapping there. They "had some words," but the other guy pulled up his traps after John informed him he had been trapping there since the first day of the season. It never dawned on John who that "other guy" with a black moustache and wearing a sheepskin troopers cap was until he got home and then realized it was Bill Nelson. They eventually got to know each other and became friends, and John visited him several times and bought some lures.

Bill and Edith lived a pretty simple life, and they didn't "want" for anything more. They used an outhouse in their back yard and there was a water well with a hand pump behind the house, too. I packed a few pails of water into the house for Edith when I visited them. They had some old, worn, basic furniture in the house and I remember they had an old black-and-white TV in their living room and Bill commenting there *"Wasn't much worth watching on it, anyway."* He would rather read or visit.

The Nelson's lived a simple life and weren't much for luxuries. Note the outhouse and hand-pump water well in their back yard shown in the upper right corner of the photo.
(Bill Nelson photo)

Bill thought a lot of his wife and affectionately referred to her as *"Mrs. Bill"* in several of his articles. She was always there by his side when he needed her and it must have been very hard for her when he was gone so much. Sonny Hootman said she had friends in town she visited with while Bill was away.

Bill and Edith did not have any children. His mother, Hannah, lived with them for several years until she passed away. Bill liked kids, though, and he would help them get started trapping, fishing, hunting, etc., if they were sincere. Sonny Hootman said that Bill "took him under his wing" as a kid, and took him trapping, hunting, and fishing. "If he liked you, he would do about anything for you," Sonny said. Years later, Sonny was driving to an area he was logging in and saw a coyote cross the road in front of him. When he returned home that evening, he stopped by Bill's to tell him about it and asked him what size trap he should use to try and catch the coyote. Bill gave him a #4 Victor jump trap with teeth welded to the jaws as well as some coyote lure. In a few days, Sonny caught the coyote. Four years ago, Sonny gave me that trap, and along with Bill's old shotgun that Don Paul gave me, are my two most prized items in my collection of Nelson memorabilia. The trap still has Bill's tag on it with his unique serial number registered by the IA Conservation Commission.

Bill took the time to enjoy life, no matter how busy he was. I already mentioned him taking mid-day breaks along his marten traplines for some hot tea, lunch, and a smoke. He also wrote about enjoying the sights and sounds of nature while he was wildcrafting. He would sometimes lay on his back, looking up at the trees and sky, and listen to the birds and other natural sounds. On hot days, he would sometimes go swimming while he was out in the field. Don Paul said while they were trapping fox, Bill would stop for lunch, every day, and they would visit while eating lunch. Sonny Hootman said Bill would always insist on stopping for a smoke before they returned home from fishing or hunting, and relive the events of the day. Bill was usually willing to drop what he was doing to go hunting or fishing, too. John Barbee said when he was visiting with Bill upstairs in his house, Bill would sometimes lay on the bed and appeared to "drift off" to another world while telling John about some of his experiences from the past. Bill "took in" everything he saw and was never in too much of a hurry to "enjoy the moment" and "smell the roses".

It was obvious that Bill was independent and he didn't like working for others. His few years at the wire factory and with the U.S. Forest Service were probably the longest periods he worked for someone else. In one of his wildcrafting articles, he wrote, "... *The feeling of independence of working for one Bill Nelson.*"

Bill was blessed with a good sense of direction which he acknowledged and was grateful for. In fact, that sense probably kept him from getting lost in adverse weather conditions, several times, and might have even saved his life. Don Paul told me when he and Bill trapped together, Bill had taught him to always pick a prominent landmark way out in front of him and use it as a guide as he proceeded in that direction. Otherwise, Bill said it was natural for people to walk in circles, thinking they were walking in a straight line. He also taught Don to look back while he was walking and recognize landmarks in that direction for the return trip. Just in case, Bill had a prearranged signal of firing 2 shots in quick succession from his pistol, to give Don a guide for finding him. Don said he did get lost one time during a very foggy morning and almost as if he expected it, Bill fired the 2-shot signal, and they reunited. Bill did not criticize or ridicule him about it, however.

Don said Bill was not afraid of any animal and when they trapped some farmer's dog, Bill would "talk it down" and release it from the trap without getting bit. Bill wrote about a couple of animal encounters he had over the years. He once trapped a large coydog that attacked him as he approached. He thought it was *"all too handsome,"* so stunned it by rapping it on the nose and released it from the trap. *"Foolish? Perhaps, but I often have such weak moments,"* he said. He also wrote, *"Believe it or not, I have walked up to a trapped 'cat and rubbed its ears and scratched its back. That 'cat made a coarse housecat-like sound when I rubbed its ears, and I felt like the devil when I finally decided that after all, I was a trapper and had to kill the critter before I could skin it."*

Bill had his "soft moments" while wildcrafting, too. He related an incident where he discovered a patch of wild ginseng that had been planted from seed by another root hunter. He backed off and left the patch alone, just in case the other hunter would ever return to reap the rewards of his efforts of planting the seeds.

One could wonder what Bill did with all the records, notes, and field diaries he kept. He wrote, *"Ever so often, I thumb through the stacks of notebooks, old composition books, and various trapline records. At times, I will scatter them around on the floor and spend hours reliving some trapline trails of the past. No few times, I have sharpened up my fur-taking ability by reading my own* notes and records. It not only allows me to read actual entries, but recalls to mind many incidents of the past. It brings to mind old favored sets that so often contributed to better-than-average fur takes. Most of all, it has added greatly to my understanding of certain animal habits, improvements in accepted methods, use of lures, applications, and the many 'little tricks' of the game."

As mentioned throughout this book, Bill used the best equipment he could afford. When I first visited him in 1969, he proudly displayed a new pair of Eddie Bauer hiking boots with vibram soles that cost $75. That was a lot of money for a pair of boots at that time, but he insisted on top quality.

Was Bill Nelson perfect? Of course not. Like all of us, he had his faults. Harry Batten said he could be "downright ornery," especially if he had too much to drink. Don Paul said that by the end of trapping season, Bill's patience wore thin and it didn't take much to "set him off." As with well-known celebrities in any field, Bill had his enemies and competitors who were jealous of him. I have written documentation from two of them I won't name, even though they're both dead. They did not have very complementary things to say about him. Not all of his competitors felt that way about him, though. Bill told me that E.J. Dailey, another famous trapper, lure maker, and author from NY, had stopped by to visit him, but Bill was out of state, trapping. E.J. left him a nice note, however, and said he was sorry to have missed meeting and visiting with him. Since this book is intended to honor Bill, I will not dwell on any more with negative things about him. It would serve no purpose.

Bill and Edith both liked dogs and he said they usually had at least one during all their years of marriage. When I visited them, they had a German police, Lobo, whom Bill sometimes affectionately called, "Lupee" (after Lupus). Lobo was friendly and quickly came to you for a pat and some attention. While sleeping on the Nelson's couch, I remember him checking on me a couple times during the night and sticking his nose close to my face. Bill said he had always done that, even with him and Edith.

Dogs seemed to bring out the soft side of Bill that few people probably knew. One of the most touching and personal articles he wrote was about his favorite dog, Bones. He acquired him as a pup from a friend a year or so before he made his first trip to CA. He named him, Bones, because he was so lean and hungry-looking that his bones actually stuck out from his body.

Lobo, one of Bill's and Edith's dogs during the 1960s. (Bill Nelson photo)

Mutt, left, and Judy, Bill's and Edith's dogs during the Sierra years and in IA.
(Photo courtesy of Marlene Rider)

They quickly bonded to each other and Bill began to take him out in the field with him. Bill believed a good dog must be somewhat spoiled. *"You just cannot get close to your dog unless you spoil him a little. I find that this can be done and still keep your controls. Bones was the best dog I ever owned in this respect. He was utterly spoiled and yet he obeyed even a whispered command from me."* Bill took Bones with him to CA and taught him how to avoid trap sets after learning the hard way and getting caught, several times. Bill also taught him to fight and kill trapped coyotes and bobcats. When they slept out in siwash camps along

Bill's favorite dog, Bones.
(Bill Nelson photo)

the trapline, Bones would not curl up to sleep, but rather stretch out, flat, next to Bill for mutual warmth. When the campfire was about out, Bones would lick Bill's face to wake him so he could put more wood on the fire. As Bill put it, "*Things like that bring a man and his dog very close. Too close, as a man knows that some day he will lose his dog.*"

Back in IA, Bones would accompany Bill to the river and learned to love swimming and chasing prey. While Bill dug mussels, Bones would swim and search out muskrat dens where he would patiently wait and ambush the muskrat as it left its den. Bones even saved Bill from a rattlesnake, one time, by barking and preventing him from going near the spot where the snake was coiled, ready to strike.

Bill said Bones was a scrapper and took on any dog, regardless of size. He eventually got a mate for Bones- Sissy, a small fox terrier that Bones grew to worship. After their first litter of pups, Bill said, "*When Bones became a father, he was quite as foolish as the average human father is over his first born. He had an abashed air about him, but present, too, was a fierce pride. He seldom went near the pups, but kept his distance and showed approval by the great swelling of his chest.*"

Bones had a way of showing his disapproval, too. Bill said, "*He had a bed in one corner of one room. Now and then, my wife would forget to shake and air his bedding. When this happened, we were both treated to a very reproachful look and he refused to sleep on it until it was properly cleaned . . . He had a way of chastising me if he felt I had done wrong. He would simply avoid and ignore me for a length of time in harmony with the extent of my crime. Later, he would forgive me and be especially attentive to let me know all was well, again. If I should come home with the aroma of alcohol too strong on my breath, I would be out of bounds, as far as he was concerned. Once, my wife and I had some sharp words while hunting relics. He must have thought I was in the wrong that time, as he gave me a bad look and followed her home. It was not until the next day that I was forgiven.*" Bill said Bones could beg, too, though. "*He was well mannered. No jumping up, barking, or crowding. He simply would sit back at a respectful distance and look at one with that soft, pleading look in his eyes. No shifting of his gaze,* just that steady look, shivering slightly, and quietly drooling at the mouth . . . He used that trick with equal success on me and others."

Bill was with Bones when he died several years later on a summer evening. "Heat lightning was flashing far to the northwest and the soft sounds of the night crept in the quiet room and kept us company. I had been sitting there for 2 hours with his head cradled in my lap. I had moved him to where we could face the open door and feel the warm fingers of the night air and listen to the gentle strumming of the crickets and the cicadas. Even then, he looked eagerly out into the darkness, and when he heard the strange harsh cry of a heron, he lifted his ears and then feebly licked my hand with that little gesture of comradeship. It must have cost him a great effort, but it was his way of saying, 'That's our world out there, and it is nice to know we are enjoying it, together.' A few minutes later, he stirred a bit, and then died in my arms. I sat there very still for a long time and his whole life story flashed across the screen of my mind . . . I stroked that fine head and then I tenderly wrapped him in the red wool coat that I had worn in the North Country and that he had so long cherished for a bed. I walked down the dark road that led to the river with his coat-wrapped form in my arms, and there in that soft warm darkness, I was a boy once more and I felt very bad about losing a friend and companion that had been with me over so many outdoor trails. When I came to the river, I sat down and rested my face on the coat and again listened to the notes of the whippoorwills and I watched the moon riding high in the sky with a veil of thin cloud drawn over its face. No grave for Bones. I placed him in the waters of the river that he loved so well. The coat allowed him to ride high and clean on the water. I pushed him into the current of the river that had seemed to mute its busy, rippling, babble of sound. I watched him fade away into the darkness and I choked out a very personal little prayer to speed him along to the portals of the great, bright hunting grounds where surely all square shooters and their dogs must go."

Back in 1957, Bill predicted, "Personally, I feel the day of the long-haired fur will dawn, again." While visiting with his old partners, friends, and colleagues, we all said it was a shame that he hadn't lived another 10 years, or so, so he could have seen his prediction come true and trapped some of those highdollared furs during the fur-boom years of the 1970s and 1980s and experienced a large increase in his lure business. Sonny Hootman explained, though, "Bill probably wouldn't have changed a bit. He was happy where he was at and with what he had. He probably couldn't have handled an increase in his business and would have been very disgusted with all the gimmicks and fly-by-nighters that appeared during those years." And so, maybe it was a blessing that Bill lived when he did, rich in the memories and experiences he had.

Bill lived life the way he wanted to and was proud to be a trapper and an outdoorsman.
(Bill Nelson photo)

Chapter 23

FINAL CHAPTER

Sometime during 1971, Bill developed cancer in his mouth, throat, and neck areas. He steadily grew worse and died at home on March 7, 1973. He was 64 and would have been 65, had he lived until his birthday on August 23rd. Harry Batten said Bill suffered a lot and died a horrible death. His funeral was held on March 10th and he is buried in the Croton Cemetery, near where he grew up and the hills and river he loved.

And so ended the great career of Bill Nelson. The full impact of his knowledge, trapping systems, lures, and writings were not fully realized and appreciated until years later. Then, he became a legend. Hopefully, this book will serve as a permanent record of the Outdoorsman Extraordinaire.

"I do not think that very many of us have ever lived and fulfilled all the boyhood dreams we have had. I have- every trapline dream, and most every plan I made."

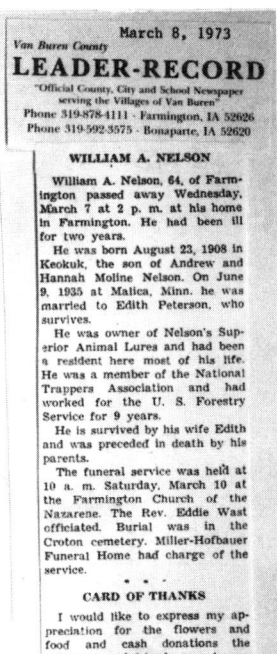

Bill's grave in the Croton, IA cemetery.
(Sherm Blom photo)

Courtesy of LEADER-RECORD

Chapter 24

EPILOGUE

Edith tried to continue Bill's lure business after his death, but it was very difficult for her, since he had always operated it. Sometime during the summer of 1973, she sold the lure business, including the current inventory of lures and ingredients, to Fuller and Ruth Laugeman from Winnett, MT. They changed the name of the business from "Nelson's Superior Animal Lures" to "Laugeman's Big Sky Lures, Nelson's Formulas," and printed a new catalog and began advertising that fall. The "Superior Animal Lures" title was later adopted by another lure maker.

Edith suffered a stroke during the spring of 1974 and was kept in a hospital in IA for 3 weeks and then transferred by her brother, Raynerd Peterson, to a nursing home in Minneapolis, MN. She remained there until her death on October 29, 1983. The Nelson house and property remained vacant until the early 1980s when it was auctioned off and purchased by a local man who then tore the house down and resold the property. Ruth Laugeman told me in a phone conversation in 1983 that a man who lived near Farmington, IA had visited their booth at the National Trappers Association convention in Hutchinson, KS that summer and told them he had attended the Nelson property auction and saw boxes and boxes of Bill's old files, papers, photos, letters, books, etc. burned because nobody had bid on them or offered to carry them away. What a tragedy it is that someone didn't keep his life-long work that he worked so hard and diligently to record and preserve.

She died October 29, 1983

Edith Nelson

NEW HOPE — Funeral services for Edith Nelson, 79, of New Hope, formerly of Clarks Grove, will be held at 2 p.m., Saturday, at Bonnerup & Son Funeral Chapel in Albert Lea. The Rev. Fred Jacobson will officiate. Interment will be in the Clarks Grove Cemetery.

Mrs. Nelson died Saturay at the Ambassador Nursing Home in New Hope.

She was born June 28, 1904, in Clarks Grove to Carl and Augusta Peterson. She was married to William Nelson in 1934.

She was a graduate of Albert Lea High School and worked as a bookkeeper at Clarks Grove Hardware for 12 years until her marriage, when the couple moved to Farmington, Iowa.

She lived in Farmington until her husband's death in 1974. She then moved to the Ambassador Nursing Home in New Hope, where she had resided since.

She is survived by two sisters, Helen Howland of Pontiac, Mich., and Verna Peterson of Clarks Grove; one brother, Raynerd Peterson of Minneapolis, and nieces and nephews.

She was preceded in death by her husband in 1973; three brothers, Fred, Charley and Emil Peterson, and two sisters, Mrs. A.J. (Alice) Logeson and Mrs. Raymond (Vesta) Wright.

Friends may call at Bonnerup & Son Funeral Chapel on Saturday one hour before the services.

**Courtesy of
Ruth Peterson**

Ruth Laugeman passed away on August 31, 1995, but Fuller continues to operate the lure business, selling Bill's lures, bait, bait solution, books, and dirt antifreeze method. He also sells 2 lures that Bill had developed, but didn't get to market, before he died. Fuller does not sell lure ingredients or the 3 units of lure formulas, however.

LAUGEMAN BIG SKY LURES
P.O. Box 209
Winnett, MT 59807-0209
Phone: 406-429-7711

His catalog can be purchased for one first-class stamp.

Today, a new house is located on the site of the old Nelson property and there is no evidence of the Outdoorsman Extraordinaire who lived there for so many years and left us his legacy.

The Nelson property in 1989 after
the house had been torn down and the property
cleared and leveled. (Sherm Blom photo)

As mentioned, Bill was interviewed by the "Des Moines Register" newspaper in 1949 and an article appeared in the Sunday edition on January 9, 1949, "Local Trapper Outfoxes The Foxes- 195 In A Month. Curiosity Draws Foxes To Investigate His Traps," by Louis Cook, Jr.

Since Bill died, there have been several tributes to, and articles written about him. These are the ones I am aware of:

"The Longliner Hall Of Fame- Bill Nelson", 1985. O'Gorman Long-Line Lures Catalog, pp 41-42. L. Craig & Dana O'Gorman. Broadus, MT.

"Legendary Trapper Bill Nelson- A Lifetime Afield From Iowa To The Sierra Nevadas", by Mike Wilson. January 1989 FUR-FISH-GAME, p 56 and Joe Goodman print drawn from photo furnished by Jack Harris.

"Trapping With Bill Nelson", by Everett Swearingen, October 1993, "FUR-FISH-GAME", P 64.

"Legendary Trapper Bill Nelson", 11"x17" Limited Edition Print. 1989. Joe Goodman Limited Edition Prints, Columbus, OH.

"Legendary Bill Nelson Remembered Fondly-Renowned Outdoorsman, Writer, Revealed As A Common Man With Uncommon Skills", by Sonny Hootman. June 1995 FUR-FISH-GAME, pp 57, 59.

Cover photo, "Bill & Edith Nelson" and article, "The Legendary Bill Nelson", by L. Craig O'Gorman. Nov/Dec TRAPPER'S WORLD, pp 15-16.

Several reprints of Bill's articles have appeared in various magazines such as FUR-FISH-GAME, AMERICAN TRAPPER, and TRAPPER' WORLD, over the years.